# MANLOBBI'S DESCENT

# JULIAN COCHRAN

---

## MANLOBBI'S DESCENT

TRANSCRIBED BY THE MODENA TOWNSFOLK

---

ROBERT BREMNER PUBLISHING

ROBERT BREMNER

Published by Robert Bremner Publishing
Australia   ACN 107 100 041
www.robertbremner.com

First published in 2016

Cochran, Julian   *Manlobbi's Descent*

ISBN-10: 0-646-95342-7 (hardcover)
ISBN-13: 978-0-646-95342-7 (hardcover)

This book has been composed in
IM FELL DW Pica PRO by Robert Bremner Publishing

Manufactured in USA

# CONTENTS

# CHAPTER 1
# MANLOBBI'S FIRST DESCENT

Hither, thou readest the book of the suffering Manlobbi endures as an uncommon, but true, invest'r. Having spoken, and the township before him having grown in prosp'rity, its people have to the full extent pass'd on his w'rds for thee, f'rtunate one, the great wealth and stimulation of the mind.

F'r twenty–years Manlobbi liv'd on the cliffs to better understand his limitations, conduct experiments, and in his emancipation, nurtur'd his aptitude f'r more heightened endeavours. For earlier, Manlobbi had come to understand that to learn knowledge was easier than to unlearn it, and from experiments with the town people and the reading of their writings, it would be faster to be aroint from them, and the stillness within the cliffs, and their heightening of his senses, provid'd the greater purity of thought.

But after many years with failings and successes,

the flood of his knowledge had risen to the brink of overflowing, and Manlobbi seek'd the consonance from passing on his findings so he could acquire more, and he descend'd from the cliffs to meet again with the common–men, and to pass these mental models upon them.

Yet, from the first day upon descending, the task proved large, as it appear'd that no–one could understand him. Furthermore, they mock'd him, and some from a distance, threw stones upon him. What the township valued had fea in common with Manlobbi, and the conversations between neighbours about his doings became interlaced with humour, which comfort'd them, f'r Manlobbi's endeavours of excellence were not understood by them, except the endeavour of generating vast wealth. This had attract'd the township's attention, and produced some scrabbling, howev'r most of the township shared stories amongst neighbours of their dread and envy towards Manlobbi, for each year he had come to own more of the township's land.

When they gather'd at night near fires to pay tribute to a myth, Manlobbi once join'd them and present'd them with knowledge. They spoke of their myth, and present'd a gift to him. But they would not hear Manlobbi's w'rds, as to face this knowledge they would risk argument with their cater–cousins. Thus the knowledge could not be bear'd. A man embracing a guitar turn'd to Manlobbi and ask'd :–

"Thou dilatest exotic things, but what dost thou wot about the taste of our cheese? Thou canst not yea describe our wine. What dost thou wot of our community?"

And the guitar wielder strummed the strings and then he sang, and the song's w'rds affirm'd the beliefs of those that surround'd him, and his followers sigh'd. Amongst these followers, a confident one spoke :–

"Behold, in this newspaper our festival cheese is betold. Thou hast read the news? Nay, thou belike readest only books of mad–men and wot fea about what goes on. Nay, thou need'st not heed our cheese. But tell me – how doth thy foreign art, and other magic thou presentest, help us? And how doth it help me? Thou believest it can sell my stock of shoes?"

And he raised his hand at Manlobbi :–

"This adorned ring doth not grow from the clouds. Canst thou see it? Yea. There are some things your magic cannot bring."

The confident one's eyes rotated to the guitar–wielder to confirm that he had also seen his hand, and with greater self–belief, continued :–

"Canst thou use a hammer? Dost thou know what a hammer is?"

The followers again sighed, and Manlobbi hence began the overflow of his knowledge.

That night, as Manlobbi walked alone through the township's streets, his inner flame flickered, and became brighter through the echo of their w'rds.

"Alas they cannot hear my words, but they hear

each other. And if they can see each other, then they will become untangled from each other. Thus I will reveal them to each other. I will present to them – themselves."

Thus Manlobbi return'd, and ov'r time, a bawbling number of the folk began to bewray comprehension, and at times a great enthusiasm. These wealthy ones came to be, but there w're only a few, and as Manlobbi, they became ridiculed by the crowd. For whilst the townsfolk want'd to be the same as those around them, there was a stronger force in that they want'd those around them to be as themselves.

As the years passed, the embolden'd ones ask'd questions of ev'ry variety, and whilst Manlobbi enjoy'd their vibrance and took joy in filling them further with knowledge, they took it upon their own initiative to inscribe the teachings to pass onto oth'rs. These inscriptions have been made as complete as the folk could comprehend, and present'd h're.

# CHAPTER 2
# THY COMPANIONLESS PATH

Being a true invest'r dost not require investing as Manlobbi, such he had exclaimed, but to have thy constant quest f'r self–criticism, acquiring knowledge, to be conscious of, yea if not ov'rcoming, our psychological biases, and improving one's art.

Being a true invest'r is lonely. No–one, 'r seldom few, will und'rstand thee, and will gen'rally distrust thy judgement, and align the observ'd great success ov'r time to luck. But w'rse, with 'r without this mockery, thou wilt have to exercise the most extreme self–control to not act, as doing naught is usually the most valuable action. The extent of patience involv'd, and resistance to influence from the surrounding idiocy, are challenges generally insurmountable.

But an immense amount of wealth is at stake, and as the amount is not intuitive the endeavour is consequently easily ignor'd. The diff'rence between a 3%

return and a 15% return ov'r 40–years is m're than eighty–fold ($1.15^{40}$ / $1.03^{40}$), and if the endeavour is repeat'd f'r another generation then the difference becomes m're than sixty–four–hundred–fold ($80^2$ = 6,400).

Why can the invest'r not simply repeat the approach of past successful invest'rs? Ay, a tiny number can, but there are pre–requisites. To invest successfully requires an extraordinarily independent mind, and yea f'r the rare case of invest'rs who have actually acquired effective methods of past successful invest'rs, they know exactly what they need to do, but cannot do it in the presence of natural forces, peer pressure and other psychological biases. Despite knowing what they must do, actually acting upon it and applying the required self–control and patience is of profound challenge. Why not, then, only mirror their purchases and sales? This creates an appearance that one will not need to make any decisions, howev'r one will nevertheless succumb to the same psychological forces and deviate from the strategy, more oft than not, near the worst possible time. (The habit of investigating the characteristics of securities purchased by these investors having an unusually excellent track record, will howev'r be beneficial.)

Throughout all social species, animals are highly affected by the thinking and actions of those animals that surround them. This social phenomenon evolved as our corses evolved, and hath thus generally been to our advantage as, for example, the wandering murderer entering the township, whence the information will be rapidly thrown upon us involuntarily. This involuntary spreading of information by word of mouth, newspapers and the internet, howev'r, and even when less urgent than the wandering murderer, leads to interesting distortions that will not import those of most endeavours, but must particularly import the invest'r.

This information–spreading within the crowd must be likened to a virus contagion, having the identical mathematical characteristics for its expansion and collapse. Whilst the information contagion allows more rapid attention to important matters, and enormously reduces the aggregate effort required for everyone to learn this information, interesting distortions also occur, as concerns the true invest'r. The crowd–members turn each of their heads in the same direction at once, thus there is an appearance of increasing the amount of information per mazzard, but there is much less effortful enquiry. This leads to a distortion of the facts, compar'd to if the facts were individually researched, thus the *correct* information per mazzard is oft decreased (for example, the murderer, upon approaching him, could be found to be gentle and his unfamiliar attire had start'd rumours). With everyone looking in the same direction, the contagion also reduces the diversity of attention variety, and in combination with the less correct information, this more massively decreases the aggregate correct information throughout the whole the crowd.

The spreading mechanism of the contagion itself can lead to further distortions, such as by word–of–mouth variation and selective media reporting (for example the rumours of the man's attire becoming increasingly exaggerated, and his perceived motives interpreted increasingly factually). These distortions lead to many problems for the invest'r, but the three main problems are as follows:

Firstly, the crowd causes thy purchases to be made at the wrong time. The narrow attention of the crowd combin'd with the massive weight of repetition of that attention multiplied through the population, and occurring at the same time, affects the stock quotations corresponding to that attention. Multiple positive feedback effects involving the crowd exaggerate this further, as expanded upon in chapter 13.

Secondly, the crowd causes thy purchases to be made upon the wrong security. The crowd will produce myths, and distortions of facts, that, unlike avoiding the murderer which is either neutral 'r beneficial, will cause the invest'r to place his attention not only towards the wrong security but also towards untrue facts about the security yea in the case that thou had independently selected it.

Thirdly, the influence of the crowd is involuntary, regardless of how strong one's will is to avoid its influence, as illustrat'd by it being impossible to not wot of the wandering murderer within the township. Furthermore there is no immediately perceiv'd penalty f'r succumbing to the crowd, and this greatly weakens the incentive to avoid its influence. The penalty occurs only many years later through the inferi'r result that ensues.

The true invest'r hath develop'd methods that function as a barrier to lower these crowd–effects. The gross–in–sense practical methods involve avoiding of newspapers, except when 'tis not popular amongst invest'rs or f'r the purpose of providing entertainment, and more generally avoiding all information that is transmit'd for large populations of invest'rs. Most effectively, he will recognise the importance of his natural capacity f'r seeking information from his own fancy, individual interests, and from his own initiative. He will furthermore attempt to nurture a habit of independent thinking, a skepticism towards popular ideas, and an active and more effortful enquiry of facts. Regarding the true investor's location, living in a village will give better results than living in the financial district of Lower Manhattan. Whilst populous areas do generally not need to be regard'd as harmful, they will be avoid'd particularly whence there are many discussions of finance. As with the newspapers, a stance of taking this information as entertainment when 'tis *provid'd* to thee, rather than *request'd* by thee, will temper its harmful mental impact.

Howev'r, even with these methods to avoid the crowd's financial harmfulness, in order to appreciate the immensity of the task at hand the true invest'r may liken the crowd to the ocean, where his task is to keep his mazzard above the ocean surface in order to avoid drowning. Like the crowd, the ocean nev'r disappears and it must be accepted that one's avoidance of its effects can only be a continual and effortful pursuit, with the avoidance of drowning nev'r fully overcome.

Whilst the true invest'r is nev'r freed from the crowd's down–pulling, he will howev'r be resolv'd to

study its characteristics and effects. 'Tis in this studious
and curiosity–fill'd pursuit that he will become slightly
lighten'd upon the ocean, and provid'd with significant
advantage f'r superi'r results in the endeav'r of investing.
This lightening of the effects, howev'r, must not be
automatically assum'd to be achievable. One will be wiser
to assume some amount of drowning within the ocean as
unavoidable and the task thus to merely reduce one's
drowning in part.

# CHAPTER 3
# WHAT DOTH A TRUE INVEST'R
# DO EACH DAY?

Nearly all his time is reading, and largely past and present annual reports, but also studying industries of interest, according to his caprice and will, and generally acquiring knowledge. This is what makes a pure invest'r.

As Manlobbi had ask'd, what dost an auth'r of a novel do? The act is to create, so one might think that they might not but sit down and write? But this is not true. They will not act, that is, write, f'r the majority of time. Their time is consum'd by conducting life itself, thinking about their subject, reading with subjects relating to and not relating to the novel, introspection and pondering.

Likewise, investing involves only thinking, and not doing aught. If thou hast an urge to see the result of thy actions, in relief of this teen of impatience, then thou wilt tend to make irrational decisions, and ov'r time fail

thy pursuit as an invest'r. Thou mak'st purchases and
sales of portions of companies fairly rarely, say twice a
year, and thou lay–to a discount brokerage f'r the
transaction. So the rest of the time is reading and
thinking. Some far smaller time writing letters to
management, 'r to acquaintances with familiarity with
the industry, 'r speaking informally with customers of
the business being investigat'd. But one's reading and
thinking is not only about prospective companies to buy,
and in fact most of it isn't. One pursues knowledge in all
domains, and celebrates creative self–criticism and
criticism of one's decisions.

The writings about finance by common–men, the
writings of self–help books and claims that investing
successfully is aught other than extraordinarily difficult,
should largely be view'd as destructive to thy knowledge,
and to thyself, as it introduces falsehoods. These
charlatan ponderings, with empty assertions,
shepherding techniques and other comforting, not only
destroy thy will and capacity to succeed in this particular
endeavour, but furthermore require energy to unlearn,
f'r unlearning requires more energy than learning. So
thy reading becomes highly selective, as we are selective
about the quality of air we breath and avoid hideous
odors. The terrible od'r from most writings similarly
should be felt, and act'd upon by avoiding them. But the
writings of all businessmen should not be overlook'd as
we want to seek their weakness in contribution to whe'r
their business should be ignor'd.

The invest'r must not forget that he is an owner
of each business purchas'd in part, whe'r one share or a

large portion of the company is owned, and he is consequently entitled to ask the management any reasonable question, for which the Investor Relations will provide their contact details. If the management cannot answer a question then they are obliged to provide a legitimate reason as to why. But whilst having the mindset of a pragmatic business owner, the true invest'r is nevertheless largely an observer. He may advise his management, tour their premises and provide his votes over corporate matters using proxy forms, however these are not the most consequential activities. The true invest'r votes far more consequentially with his decision to allocate capital towards, and away from, the security. His heedful selection of an excellent partner is recognised as more effective than the attempt to change his partner.

The endeavour of investing requires capital in addition to the expansion of capital. The true invest'r, in seeking capital, also benefits by working within various businesses, 'r yea better, creating his own business from first–principles. The hardship and experience of pursuing his own business endeavours will greatly improve his own judgement of other businesses.

# CHAPTER 4
# THY BASELINE

If ye are to pursue the endeavour of investing, thou wilt wish to wot how to measure thy virtue. Owing to random fluctuations, thy excellence can only be measur'd ov'r a period of time exceeding three–years at the extreme and less–than–reliable minimum, five–years at a reasonable minimum, and seven–years to have a realistic indication of whe'r thou hast achiev'd thy aim. Furthermore, this period of time should have the starting and ending points of the general market in a similar humour, and whe'r pessimistic, euphoric 'r neutral, the starting and ending points in which thou measurest thy returns should be of approximately the same humour and spirit.

Given this, what will betoken that thou hast met thy target? 'Tis common–sense that if someone had done naught other than invest in a low cost index fund, and outperform'd thy full–time enterprise, then thou must be seen as a daw.

Verily, the vast majority of the industry hath this foolish category, with manag'd funds underperforming their respective index out of mathematical necessity and thus in the empirical record.[1] But the manag'd funds industry's past, present and future failure is not a reason to not strictly expect outperformance by thyself. For a fool amongst fools is treated kindly by these daws, but is still a daw. So thy baseline needn't be the performance of these daws.

Thou canst furthermore set thy benchmark yea higher than both the low cost index funds and the managed funds. There are a variety of mechanical investment strategies that automatically choose a subset of all businesses in the broad market, by various criteria, which effectively define a new index fund. F'r example, an index that remains invest'd in the 10% of 500 largest businesses having the highest earnings yield, 'r having

---

[1] Index funds were compar'd to their like–for–like manag'd funds having a minimum 10–year history as track'd by the Lipper subsidiary of Thomson Reuters Company. In the 10–year period ending December 31 2015, 10 of 10 money market funds, 49 of 52 bond funds, 18 of 18 balanced funds, and 109 of 122 stock funds underperform'd the respective Vanguard index fund. The 10–ten year period of outperformance by some manag'd funds will be inevitable owing to randomness, howev'r the administration costs of running a fund will provide an ongoing drag below the index. Manag'd funds underperform 'r outperform, but in aggregate must match the index 'ere their costs, with the vast majority of capital manag'd institutionally. 'Tis a practical consequence that the longer the comparison study is extended, the larger the ratio of underperforming manag'd funds to the total number becomes, until we eventually will observe not a single diversified manag'd fund outperforming their respective index. In short, the industry of manag'd funds is as useful as paying a man to walk behind thee carrying thy wallet, and the public, on aggregate, would be wealthier if they permitt'd the industry of diversified manag'd funds (including the higher expense funds posing as speciality index funds) to vanish by selecting only low–cost index funds.

the highest quotation increase ov'r the past year. A number of these strategies, including these two, have proven to outperform the broad market marginally ov'r the long–term. This is bewray'd by long backtests and further supported by some, though invariable lesser, continued outperformance when equity is genuinely commit'd to the simplest strategies with the longest backtests – 30–years an absolute minimum – with studious attention to eliminating data–mining biases. Howev'r the important four observations are as follows: Firstly the actually realised outperformance of these mechanical investment strategies is gentle, such as 3% per–year at the high range, as can be reasonably statistically determin'd. Secondly, these strategies are extremely difficult to follow consistently because negative results will occur f'r a long series of years, and these results affect the historical record originally justifying their lay–to. Thirdly, the ongoing realisation of permanent losses, as falling stocks are sold, makes these strategies psychologically very difficult to follow, resulting in a negative performance bias from moving away from models with recent weak performance to models of recent strong performance. Fourthly, which will later permit this chapter's conclusion, the vast majority of this outperformance is achiev'd by the simple fact that the funds are investing in each business with capital in equal proportions, known to many as equal–weight–indexing. Howev'r a pure equal–weight–index already hath been shown to outperform the standard broad market index, such as the S&P500, a capitalisation–weight'd index, by about 2% per–year and about 1.5% net–of the additional taxation. Consequently, 'tis sound to ignore these mechanical investing strategies and simply invest in an equal–weight index to achieve a long–term return 1.5% ahead of the standard index invest'rs, likewise without exercising ongoing research.

It is a jovial application of common–sense that this out–performance by the equal–weight index is furthermore rationally expect'd, f'r both economic and, separately, mathematical necessity. In the case of the mathematical, the larger capitalisation is partly explain'd by overvaluation, rather than simply the larger economic business size, and so the equal–weight index doth not fall victim f'r this over–exposure to the expensive. F'r the economic case, the smaller firms do not suffer from market supply saturation and pragmatic inflexibility as the larger firms do.

So it might be taken that our benchmark is an equal–weight–index. We should firstly examine all the possibilities by observing the long–term returns, in each case comparing the investment results ov'r 214–years[2] f'r all assets, except real estate which is measur'd ov'r 146–years. The equal–weighted index average return was derived using 30–year Value Line data. [3]

---

2        J. Siegel, *Stocks for the Long Run* (McGraw–Hill, 1994)

3        The 1.8% advantage of equal–weight index over the market–cap weight index (S&P500) was derived by the author using data from Value Line. The nominal CAGR of 9.7% for S&P500 including dividends compares to the nominal CAGR of 11.5% for equal–weight allocations of the largest 500 companies with monthly rebalancing including dividends, both indexes compar'd over the period 1986 to 2016. This 1.8% advantage for the equal–weight index over 30–years was add'd to the long–term S&P500 return of 6.7% for the 8.5% figure shown. The advantage of equal–weight is further increased if moving from the largest 500 stocks to the largest 2,000, with a 14% CAGR from 1986 to 2016. Stock data from Value Line. Back–testing using the Screen Builder from *Jamie Gritton's MI Backtester*, www.backtest.org.

Real (inflation adjusted) average annual returns –
– inclusive of income but 'ere taxation:

| | |
|---|---|
| Common–stocks, equal–weight'd: | 8.5% |
| Common–stocks, market–cap weight'd: | 6.7% |
| Real–estate: . approximately | 3.5% |
| Bonds: . . . | 3.5% also |
| Treasury–bills: . . . | 2.7% |
| Gold: . . . | 0.6% |
| US–dollar: . . . | –1.4% |

'Tis valuable to average the annual returns ov'r such a long time–range, f'r the purpose of indicating the fundamental characteristic of each asset class, as the returns ov'r individual decades deviate greatly from the broader averages. Thirty–year intervals, howev'r, suffice to be indicative of these comparative results.[+]

Manlobbi hath emphasized that the real–estate real return of 3.5% hath factor'd the gross income yield of 5% which is reduced by 2% f'r maintenance–expenses and annual maintenance taxes, and real capital gains being 0.5%[5]. As with all of the asset classes, the capital

---

[+]      Bonds and common–stock (plus dividend) returns were compar'd using data between 1926 and 2002. F'r holding periods of 1–year, bonds outperform'd stocks 37% of the time, 12% of the time f'r 10–year holding periods, less than 1% of the time f'r 20–year holding periods and not f'r any of the 30–year holding periods. Pu Shen, *How Long Is a Long–Term Investment?* (Federal Reserve Bank of Kansas City, 2005), Chart 4.

[5]      R. Shiller, *Irrational Exuberance*, Second Edition (Princeton University Press, 2006)

gains are tax'd based on the nominal gain, rather than the real (inflation–adjusted) gain. The results actually realised are thus considerably lower f'r not only the higher performing but also the lower performing asset classes. The gold asset class, notably, hath endur'd a negative real return over the 214–years once capital-gains taxation is account'd f'r from the higher nominal return prior to subtracting inflation.

The variety of returns will have fea or no bearing on what occurs with each asset class from one year to the next, n'r when comparing periods of two– or three–years, howev'r by looking at periods of twenty–, or certainly thirty–years and holding the assets diversely, 'r an index presenting each class, then the relative performance of each asset class will resemble fairly closely the figures as above.

The true invest'r will not merely compare investments by their asset class, but by which individual situation constitutes the most prosperous return. He takes advantage of individual opportunities throughout all asset classes, for (i) the prospects for individual situations will differ considerably from the prospects of the whole class, and (ii) the relative attractiveness of each class will furthermore vary as fashions change.

F'r those that cannot pursue investing with great rigour, and if the investment timeframe exceeds twenty–years, then the first category – stocks with an equal–weight index – should be not merely their benchmark, but also the continued habit f'r holding of all of their capital, provid'd it can be held f'r as long as twenty–years. Investment horizons smaller than twenty–years, as desired by this common–folk, is not a subject that will be given attention. Except that, yea in the case of capital that remains upon the death of its owner, the function of the capital can be assum'd to be valuable beyond their mere mortality. Particularly when large amounts of capital are manag'd, the capital can be put to long–term lay–to such as the running of long–term projects requiring capital expenditure, 'r ongoing contributions to specific philanthropic causes desir'd by the original owner, such as space travel, medical research 'r public invigoration from art. Furthermore, one doth not know, with the increase in health standards, how corky one may live, and wiser to assume the longest life plausible f'r the subject of one's investment approach.

Consequently, even f'r those investing with an index, 'tis healthy to think beyond one's mortality, to emphasize the function of investing as long–term endeavour. If death occurs sooner, then it will not have holp in any case if the shorter–horizon asset classes were emphasized.

The invest'rs returns from one year to the next, and furthermore from periods spanning an entire decade, despite the individual security returns varying greatly from the underlying index, will nevertheless be buoy'd upwards and downwards by the index. This movement is similar in unpredictability to a stormy ocean, but slow'd down by a fact'r of a quarter–billion, so that at any instance the storm is not seen to be moving from our limit'd perception.

Consequently the committ'd invest'r must use, as their benchmark, this most highly performing equal–

weight–index. With prolong'd evidence of his inability to outperform 'r even match the performance of this index, such as four–years, and lacking the fortitude to improve his art, including the psychological suitability to the endeavour, he should forfeit the majority of the capital to the equal–weight–index whilst managing a smaller portion of the whole, f'r this will give more time f'r the improvement of his excellence.

# CHAPTER 5
# HOW INVESTMENTS
# SHOULD BE HELD

Investments should, as a practical summary, always be held as the common–stock, using a discount broker.

Margin debt should nev'r be utilized, even in a small proportion. The reason is that margin debt exposes thee to risk of losing the entire capital, yea with a 10% debt position, in the nonce of temporarily massive quotation declines. The benefit offer'd by the debt is extraordinarily meagre in relation to the liability in the case of this callable debt. The probability of a 90% quotation decline across thy entire portfolio appears very small, howev'r it hath come close to this in the past, and the possibility exists f'r larger declines at some point through thy remaining life. The important observation is that the decline only needs to be momentary, and the debt will be recall'd. Furthermore, new legislation 'r broker requirements could at any time request capital recall, and typically this will occur at the least opportune time, and thou wilt have no power to not comply.

Furthermore, the invest'r is generally aware of the above risks, but fails to appreciate the hidden liabilities that ensue, ironically, from this awareness itself. The debt position reduces the investor's patience (a quality to be treasured and protected) because of the interest rate drag increasing their need for more consistent and more rapid quotation rises. This reduced patience leads to a heightened attention upon the quotation. The invest'r then departs from the rational purchase and sale decisions that would have formerly applied without the debt, with new legitimately rational decisions taking their place, which subtly lead to losses. The losses are not necessarily over the entire security position, but over the surplus capital raised when the debt was undertaken, negating the purpose of the conservatively intended debt strategy. For example, the invest'r voluntarily reduces the debt during an early stage of a market decline to ensure that a future margin–call is avoided, but nevertheless still produces a permanent loss. The theoretical advantage of the debt position – when the centrally expect'd return clearly exceeds the interest rate drag – is howev'r, over the passage of a whole career, more than cancelled out by these hidden liabilities.

The capital available to invest can, howev'r, be extend'd using debt only under the condition that the debt is uncallable, which almost exclusively implies mortgage debt, unless alternatively by a special contractual arrangement, and then only if the debt interest is substantially below the annualized long–term increase in intrinsic value (plus dividends) of the holdings.

The third alternative to extend capital to invest is to mirr'r the returns of the common–stock, partly leverag'd, by holding call–options instead of the common–stock. The purchase of two–year–deep–in–the–money–call–options is vastly superior to the lay–to of margin debt. Firstly, the mapping f'r common–stock returns to the call–option returns, with the strike price at half the current quotation, is usually very similar to the mapping of common–stock returns to the 2x leverag'd margin loan returns. Secondly, the call–options do not expose thee to capital being recalled, except momentarily after 2–years as the option expires. This contrasts with margin loans where the capital can be called at any point in time. Thou canst thus be expos'd to terribly poor mis–pricings, and wait f'r the recovery, which is a luxury that thou dost not have with margin loans. Thirdly, the maximum loss f'r call–options is the equity used to purchase the options, whilst the maximum loss f'r a margin–loan is unbound'd because thou couldst be forc'd to liquidate all of the common–stock with a quotations near zero and resulting proceeds beneath the debt level.

From Manlobbi's experimental analysis, howev'r, despite these advantage of call–options ov'r margin debt, yea the most sound strategy f'r representing a holding of common–stock using call–options provides no long–term benefit to simply holding the common–stock.

# CHAPTER 6
# THE CROWD'S QUIVERING

The view towards risk by most who name themselves invest'rs is severely at odds with the way in which Manlobbi had conclud'd that risk should be view'd and consequently act'd upon. The concept of risk throughout the act of investing might not but be carefully defin'd. Risk of what? As we learn more from examining falsehoods than by confirming what we believe to be true, Manlobbi proceed'd with the three examples of falsely observ'd risk, as follows:

( 1 ) The first err'r of thinking is that common–men believe that the event to avoid is the falling in the quotation of their securities. Whe'r 'r not this sense of risk believ'd consciously, 'r yea admittedly to their neighbours, 'tis regardlessly felt, involuntarily, as whence the risk lies. The falling of the quotations is taken as the outcome that must be avoided, and thus the definition of risk is to avoid the falling of these quotations. Stop–loss strategies, in which the stock is

sold when it falls below 5%, or 20%, to prevent further
losses, are at times consider'd attractive by these
speculators, charlatan invest'rs, and inexperienced ones,
in the attempt to reduce their exposure to this risk. The
point is that these common–men have quotation declines
at the forefront of their mind – this is the subject of their
risk, and so the subject of their actions – and so they will
do everything to avoid quotation declines. ( 2 ) The
second err'r of thinking, in how risk is defined, is that
risk is in their notion view'd as something that can be
accepted, provid'd 'tis confin'd to a bawbling part of the
portfolio. Moreov'r the common–stock quantity may be
only a pittance portion of the portfolio f'r a particularly
large risk 'r whence the subject is unknown. This err'r is
more understandable and easier to rationalize, as surely
the smaller position is safer than the larger position,
howev'r Manlobbi will dilate wherefore it is verily an
err'r. ( 3 ) The third err'r of thinking is that the usual–
man, at some subconscious level, and at times
consciously, treats the falling quotation of any security –
owned 'r not owned – as having increas'd the riskiness of
the investment. If the stock was own'd during the
decline, then firstly, the sense of its riskiness is increas'd.
Secondly, a stock holding that hath the quotation
moving more frequently or agitatedly is consider'd more
risky than a less volatile, that is, a highly gentle stock
quotation.

These views of risk are not merely irrelevant to
risk, but all three perceived–risks are in the opposite
direction to the actual–risks. The investor's own
response to these mis–perceiv'd views would actually
increase, not decrease, the risk of permanent capital loss.

'Tis of fundamental importance, prior to understanding how this is evident, to require separating conceptually the business' intrinsic value and its stock price quotations. F'r verily, their compliment extern of being align'd is a mirage. When the stock declines, the psychological attention – amongst these invest'rs and their surrounding meiny, and the newspapers that they produce – shifts towards negative stories, and so it appears that the price is following a decline in the business' prospects, whence as nothing hath chang'd except the attention of the observers. The causation is perceiv'd as chang'd value leading to chang'd quotes, but in fact the causation is chang'd quotes leading to a perceiv'd chang'd value.

It may hence be explain'd wherefore these three notions of risks are errors of judgement. In the <u>first case</u>, we are interest'd in the stock quotation exceeding the intrinsic value as we have determin'd at least ten–years hence. This will invariably be a much higher level than the present level. During our endeavour of waiting patiently, the stock quotation will change frequently, particularly in amounts in the range of –20% to 25%, but notwithstanding far larger changes more frequently than one expects, from one year to the next. These smaller quotation changes do not interest us, as we wish to profit considerably from the large gain that will ensue further into the future. A temporary decline in the quotation should not serve as a distraction to our patience. Furthermore, if we were to sell a stock upon the quotation falling, such as with a stop–loss strategy, then we will have executed the action precisely in opposition to our intention, which is to sell it at a much higher quotation. 'Tis nothing more than a lack of patience, 'r poor preparation of the selection, that hath caus'd the realised loss. The investor's lack of patience, which triggered the selling at a lower price, will also be heighten'd and more difficult to resist if the preparation was poor 'r incomplete.

In the risk misjudgement of the second case, 'tis oft assum'd by the invest'r that certain stocks have higher returns but a higher chance of failure (this is made worse by the practiced mathematical analysis in modeling investment risk by the extent of the volatility of the quotation changes, rather than by the security's economic prospects). This charlatan thinking of higher–returns–equals–higher–risk, combin'd with the excitement of not knowing the future of a company and imagining a larger and colourful range of outcomes, even leads the invest'r to believe that stocks with unknown prospects hath a range of returns that are mostly higher than those from the more predictable companies. The invest'r hath learn'd from experience that they oft lose money by investing with such companies, and they have heard from the crowd the importance of diversifying their holdings. Consequently, they continue to invest in these unknown companies, but limit their exposure to a tiny part of their portfolio, such as 2% f'r each position, perhaps covering 20% of the portfolio after ten such positions are found. Their belief is that by reducing the exposure, and purchasing many companies of this risky characteristic, the aggregate risk is almost eliminated. The problem is with the premise. There is a presumption that the central expect'd return, for the average of these unknown companies, is assumed to be above the market average. It is true that some will outperform the market, but the bias will be towards underperformance rather than outperformance, and consequently taking the aggregate will not help this average result. The invest'r cannot possibly understand so many companies with a great amount of depth, and so the purchases are made oft at the overpric'd level. Moreover, the invest'r succumbs to changing news stories more readily with these lesser known companies, and with a poorer understanding of these companies, hath a tendency to buy and sell them at precisely the wrong time. Consequently the 20% allocation of the portfolio considerably underperforms the rest of the portfolio with the well understood situations, if not in the first instance then ov'r the course of the investor's career. The invest'r would be better serv'd by purchasing exactly nothing of these unknown companies, but pursuing research upon them, and holding far fewer investments in total, each well understood and generally not exceeding five situations.

'Tis common–sense that a bag containing a variety of toxic earth samples, even with some small portions of excellent soil, will on the whole remain polluted and of lower quality than the large bag of energetically select'd fertile soil, after disregarding a great number of other fine, but less excellent, bags. Withal, this strategy of holding odorous debris, but in tiny proportions, creates a habit of distemperature that is dangerous to the purity of the true investor's psychology and limit'd concentration for more commit'd investigations.

In the third case of risk misjudgement, if a

company falls in quotation, one will confirm'd that the intrinsic value hath remained approximately the same. In this case, it should firstly be common–sense that the investment was more risky before the fall than after the fall. Secondly, a stock with higher volatility which hath the quotation below the intrinsic value, will have a higher likelihood of the price more rapidly rising to intersect with the intrinsic value. Consequently the risk of the quotation remaining lower for a prolong'd period (with an opportunity–loss upon that capital) is higher in the case that the stock is less volatile. Thus, provided the security is not overpriced, the higher quotation volatility implies a lower risk to the invest'r.

So these three cases of perceived risk are liable to lead to actions by the invest'r that result in more capital loss than if the fictitious notions of risk had been ignor'd. The subconscious nature of these risk perceptions, howev'r, make them difficult to ignore, and they are best remedied by a more thorough investigation of the underlying mechanisms as discuss'd in the chapters hence.

To truly reduce risk, the intrinsic value calculation couldst be adjust'd very heavily downwards with the slightest lack of sense in the clarity of intrinsic value, howev'r the true invest'r will usually prefer a complete boycott of such an investment. Generally if a business is select'd in which the intrinsic value ten–years hence is highly predictable, then this attribute will not change abruptly ov'r many years, by the definition of it being predictable in the first place. Our task in eliminating risk is thus confin'd to the security selection, in the first place, of a business in which intrinsic value ten–years hence is profoundly predictable because of various characteristics of the individual business.

# CHAPTER 7
# THE STEADFASTNESS FILTER

The concept of *steadfastness* is central to the Manlobbi method, and the first characteristic that is search'd f'r 'ere valuation analysis proceeds. Steadfastness will be defined, f'r the purpose of investing, as having no tolerance for the asset carrying economic risk.

To be more clear, it refers to as any asset, which could be a common–stock, privately own'd asset such as a water dam, or aught that produces earnings, having no chance of the normalized earnings produced from the asset declining below the expect'd level.

The question of the steadfastness is without a formulae and must be decided with independent reasoning f'r each situation. Howev'r, the general conditions for steadfastness must be described so that we know our aim.

An income–producing security is steadfast if, both:

1. It is believed that there is no chance of the normalized earnings produced from the asset throughout the future declining below the expect'd level.

2. Whilst earnings are to be highly predictable in this way for the first 20–years, they must further have no chance of catastrophic decline for the first 40–years.

The steadfastness characteristic relates to the robustness of the earnings at any time in the future in relation to the expect'd earnings at that time, that is, the outcome reliably matching the expectation. If an asset is expect'd to have earnings ov'r the next two decades averaging $10 per–share and $20 per–share, then it would not be steadfast if the earnings remain at the $10 per–share average level. Conversely, if the asset is expect'd to have the earnings ov'r the next two decades averaging, in the consecutive decades, $10 per–share and $8 per–share, and as the two decades pass the asset marry meets these figures, then the asset must positively be consider'd to have been steadfast.

If it was thought that over a longer 40–year view, the business's characteristics exposed it to the risk of significant deterioration, then even in the event of these first two decades ensuing and having met or exceeded the investor's expectations, the investment should not have been considered steadfast from the outset.

The status of steadfastness cares nothing about whe'r earnings, n'r any other crucial economic characteristic, will decline, remain equal, 'r increase ov'r time. Steadfastness doth not import the economic performance. Rather, steadfastness rests purely on whe'r 'r not the important economic figures are firstly predictable, and secondly that they are highly reliable, in that they come to pass.

Steadfastness, with the inclusion of normalized earnings in the definition, also doth not care about the specific earnings in any single year matching the expectation, but concerns the level of earnings that would be obtained if temporary fluctuations were removed, to match the expectation. If one believes that the earnings in 2020 should be above $5 per share, then the expectation can be considered to have been met if the earnings between 2015 and 2025 averaged above $5 per share, or more precisely, that the smooth conceptually–drawn trend line through the middle of the earnings passes above $5 per share in 2020.

Government and corporate bonds immediately appear to have the steadfastness characteristic, howev'r on closer inspection it must be ask'd whe'r the 3–year or 10–year bonds will provide the expect'd return after the first decade hath passed, rather than only the bond's initial term. Ordinary bonds also produce only currency which may have its value decline, and thus are inherently not immune to inflation as other assets that produce products or services of relatively fixed real value. A 20–year or 30–year inflation protected bond should by most invest'rs, howev'r, surely be considered steadfast. But not so fast – on the second requirement for steadfastness, bonds still carry some risk of default, and the lower risk of permanent–loss of capital from the bonds, versus permanent–loss of capital from a steadfast common–stocks – 'r yea an index fund – is generally greatly exaggerat'd. Inflation protected US government bonds, in any case, would normally pass the steadfastness filter by most invest'rs, yea if the investment return fails to warrant selection.

Verily, the vast majority of businesses cannot sustain a reliable stream of earnings. The earnings each year may rise f'r fifteen–years, only to diminish greatly 'r disappear entirely in the twenty–fifth year. Everyone with a natural propensity f'r increasing knowledge will have a range of businesses that they are capable to understand, but most businesses have future earnings that no one can predict, owing to the dynamic and iterative nature of the way in which the ordinary society works. Let us say, though, that some situation actually turns out to have sustainable earnings over forty years. It doth not follow that this situation could have been graded as steadfast by anyone from the outset, for this would have required the earnings to also have been predictable from the outset without any hindsight. If we next consider this even smaller proportion of companies that can each be actually grant'd as steadfast by *someone* within the world (figure 1: shaded region), then a vastly smaller proportion again will fall under thy own domain of knowledge and insight as to be predictable by thyself. It is only this latter minute portion of situations that permit the steadfast status. Common–investors enlarge the perceived boundary surrounding these situations, whilst the true invest'rs, more conscious of their ignorance, control and yea try to squeeze this boundary smaller to only just cover the few truly comprehended situations. This acknowledgement of ignorance forms much of the spirit of identifying steadfast securities.

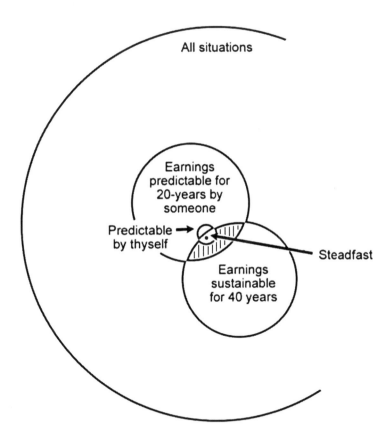

*Figure 1.*
*Rarity of steadfastness, where "predictable" means*
*normalized earnings remain above expect'd level.*

Those endeavouring to invest have shown, early in their career, a tendency to believe that all businesses that attract them, are – as granted by will and by magic – steadfast, or if they are not steadfast, then this characteristic is of meagre importance. From their results that ensue, the same invest'rs later in their career eventually move towards a tendency to believe that steadfastness is a characteristic that cannot be found, 'r when found, they continue to underestimate the amount to which it should provide a higher appraisal of the investment's merit. Consequently they settle f'r businesses without this steadfast characteristic, 'r consider those with it to be more inferi'r than the passing of time reveals.

The investor's appraisal of steadfastness closely functions with one of the most important concepts within investing: The judgement of a business can always be skipp'd. If thy employer requests that thou judgest a business, then thou wilt be forc'd to provide an analysis, yea if thou dost not understand it. Yet, as a true invest'r, thou hast the capacity to simply skip the appraisal in the case that thou canst not predict the future earnings of the business. Verily, this optionality hath a profound value, although, because of the lack of associat'd action, other than simply skipping it, the value of this optionality is invariably underestimat'd. In the general case of selecting less predictable investments, the thought of being able to skip the appraisal dost not seem exciting nor, perhaps, yea enter one's mind. The force of repulsion from its lack of steadfastness is outweighed by the force of attraction from its bright future. But in the case of committing to seek a steadfast investment, we can make use of this optionality by skipping a great number of situations before arriving at our goal. This requires greater effort pri'r to each individual purchase, and strongly implies a smaller number of holdings.

As the stringency of steadfastness is ponder'd and increasingly comprehended, it begins to appear that such a quality is unlikely to be found in common–stocks. But the examples of steadfast businesses are more frequent than the invest'r permits his awareness. They lie 'ere his blinking eyes, whilst he drifts his attention past them. The searching invest'r is skeptical of the merits of an investment that appears to be straight–forward, and is attract'd to the mystical and the unknown, f'r it better stimulates his imagination. But these steadfast investments can be found, and the strenuousness in identifying them should not cause the willful invest'r to give up the attempt and move to lesser understood alternatives f'r the sake of reducing effort.

Having defined the steadfast characteristic, and how oft' is the lack of attention towards it, we will write how Manlobbi hath spoken of its function and importance to the true invest'r. The two chapters hence provide more details about how steadfastness can be identified.

## Steadfastness purpose

The purpose of steadfastness is four–fold. Without understanding the reasons f'r this aim, the invest'r will become tired or distracted, or otherwise will  turn his attention to other matters during the attempt to identify steadfast situations. To make the matter more complicat'd, the companies without this steadfast status can oft be more exciting to explore, because the possibilities f'r their future more greatly stimulate the imagination and create interesting discussions with his neighbors, which themselves further amplify the attention.

*No permanent loss of capital:* Firstly, as the most gross–in–sense point regarding the purpose of steadfastness, by identifying and purchasing only the steadfast business, thou wilt be less expos'd to permanent loss of capital. A steadfast security will have temporary, and even prolonged, quotation declines without the intrinsic value decline, whilst the non–steadfast company will occasionally experience a significant intrinsic value decline or collapse, for which no amount of waiting will help the invest'r.

*Market inefficiency:* Earnings in the distant future, such as the 20$^{th}$ year, tend to be not thought aught about, and the likelihood of companies surviving f'r 20– years without colossal earnings declines is greatly overestimat'd. The conditions of the business in the 20$^{th}$ year might seem unimportant by the casual observation, howev'r what tends to be forgotten is that when the investment community is viewing the company from the 10$^{th}$ year, they will be looking out thither the 20$^{th}$ year. If the business prospects are to decline considerably by the 20$^{th}$ year, then invest'rs in the 10$^{th}$ year will assign a much lower earnings multiple. Consequently, when calculating the intrinsic value in the 10$^{th}$ year, it becomes important to assume a very low earnings multiple. This greatly reduces the attractiveness of the investment in comparison to a business that is known to retain earnings reliably into the 20$^{th}$ and 30$^{th}$ year, and the terminal earnings multiple can be assum'd to remain high.

If the investor's elaborate house was known to be crumpl'd and become without lay–to after 10–years, 'tis f'r this invest'r common–sense that the purchase should be either avoid'd 'r purchas'd at a vastly lower price. Without regard for symmetry, the same invest'r will appraise a common–stock with this same fragility, by lacking the similar discounting of the asking–price, n'r paying attention to importance of the value being reliable in this tenth–year with the same vigor.

*Psychological capacity*: The third purpose of requiring steadfastness is the least understood, but perhaps the most powerful, and relat'd to avoiding an overlook'd psychological bias experienc'd by invest'rs and speculators alike. In purchasing companies that are not steadfast, their returns are reduced yea in the case that they are accurate in appraising the future of the unpredictable company. Simply knowing that the company is not predictable generates a problem f'r the invest'r. If the invest'r knows that the company is utterly predictable, then this allows him to take advantage of quotation changes by purchasing stock during declines and selling the stock during rises with quotations exceeding intrinsic value.

When the steadfast filter hath not been applied, even if the central estimate of the intrinsic value hath been accurately appraised, the investor's own convictions about the economic prosperity will change through time and they will have a larger tendency to be more optimistic during quotation rises and pessimistic during declines, along with the rest of the market–participant's sentiments. These invest'rs will then inadvertently fall victim of buying high and selling low without being entirely conscious of this, 'r at least the tendency will hamper returns. The invest'r in this situation also confuses price changes with actual business–prospect changes, particularly as the price changes are reinforc'd with news–stories. Businesses with meandering future prospects will lead to loss–making trading decisions that appear rational at the time.

*Stability (of intrinsic value):* The fourth purpose of steadfastness is similar to the third in that it relates to the investor's strategic capacity to take better opportunity of quotation changes, howev'r for a different reason. Unlike the purely psychological advantage, the invest'r also benefits from the inherent characteristic of intrinsic value actually remaining stable. The intrinsic value of steadfast securities will have only min'r variations, dwarf'd by the psychologically induc'd price changes (psychologically external to the invest'r). This guarantees that the invest'r receives an investment return exceeding even the rate in which the business is perceived to be growing. The invest'r only needs to purchase at a discount to intrinsic value and sell at a smaller discount, or even a premium to intrinsic value, with the weapon–at–hand being time and patience. This, howev'r, guarantees a favourable investment return only in the case that intrinsic value is stable.

If, to consider the contrary case, the intrinsic

value fluctuated upwards and downwards, then even if the business was immune to catastrophic failure over the long–term, the investor would be rationally triggered to make purchases and sales that occasionally resulted in permanent losses. (For example, the invest'r purchases 20% below intrinsic value, the perceived intrinsic value falls by 50% after 4 years, the quotation declines by 20%, and the investor then holds security above intrinsic value, so rationally exits at a 20% loss).

# CHAPTER 8
# LONGEVITY VERSES
# STEADFASTNESS

The notion of steadfastness should not be confused with the earnings having longevity (the earnings being durable). A fundamental aspect of competitive markets is that each business wishes to expand their earnings, and this commonly hath the effect of, sometimes yea inadvertently, compressing their competitor's earnings. Consequently invest'rs are accustom'd to identifying businesses with certain characteristics that protect their earnings from competitors, 'r from broader natural redundancy of their products 'r services (which usually anyway results in the customer's attention meandered towards an indirect competitor).

Such earnings–longevity characteristics may descend from: ( 1 ) The businesses having a well known brand name, 'r other enduring characteristic that allows them to set a higher price than their competitors, and combining this with lowering the price such that margins are in the 1–4% range. Competitors can only sell the less known product at a slightly lower price, but as the leading product already hath a low margin, the competit'r simply becomes bankrupt – or in practice, declines to enter into competition. ( 2 ) The business having a larger scale than all competitors, which provides a manufacturing cost advantage that is self–reinforcing. ( 3 ) The business hath a network of customers, or a network of manufacturers or developers, using their product 'r service, in which the network itself provides much of the value of the product 'r service and consequently cannot be reproduced by a competit'r from first–principles. This characteristic is highly self–reinforcing. ( 4 ) The customers would experience an unacceptably burdensome cost if they changed the product or service, with the cost stemming from either the customer's required organisational effort, training or time penalty.

The important observation is that whilst these characteristics of longevity are highly important for the valuation, in all cases they do not last forev'r. But whilst these durability–characteristics are nev'r permanent, they should be investigated and appraised in relation to some businesses having durability–characteristics that persist for longer than others.

Earnings longevity and steadfastness can be distinguished as: *Earnings longevity provides a competitive advantage for some period of time, but is never permanent, whilst the earnings of steadfast situations are permanent for the perspective of calculating the financial present–value.* As earnings streams are more valuable in the present than in the future, the definition of permanent hath already been qualified in requiring earnings to be highly predictable for 20 years and having no chance of catastrophic decline for 40-years.

The popular brand may still be displac'd by a second brand which is expanding its product range, at some time in the future. The large–scale manufacturer might have the product become displac'd by a superior product that requires a very different fabrication plant. The business with a network of customers providing value to the business tends to have earnings longevity of excellence, howev'r the product could become displac'd by a superior product with its own growing network of users, 'r alternatively a similar product with customers from a niche, such as lawyers, musicians, or university students, could establish yea stronger longevity within that niche 'ere expanding to englut the once larger competit'r. The product or service that requires a large switching cost could eventually become sufficiently outmoded, that a gradual movement towards competing products and services will still result in greater profitability than staying with the existing state of affairs.

The characteristic of steadfastness, by contrast, is to be defin'd as permanent, with the earnings guaranteed to follow the same path, at least rather closely, as expect'd when the purchase was made.

A private hospital asset that carries no debt will have a cash–flow that is entirely robust throughout the future, if the capital expenditure is far below the earnings. But 'tis less interesting than discussing the durability of the earnings of Facebook, Linked–in 'r

Twitter owing to their undisputed network effects of the global scale. If purchasing one of these three firms, the probability of the earnings permanently declining after twenty–years, howev'r, is considerably more likely than the chance of the hospital earnings permanently declining. The hospital asset, if the balance sheet was check'd ov'r with care, would have the possibility to be rank'd as steadfast, whilst the three social–media companies would unlikely be able to be given this status. Of importance, the earnings of the three social–media companies could not only meet, but exceed the central expectations that most invest'rs have. Howev'r the question of the central estimate of their intrinsic value is highly separate to determining whe'r they are steadfast, and these concepts might not but be separat'd. Merely the potential f'r a catastrophic decline in earnings, yea if this decline dost not ensue, must merit revoking the steadfastness characteristic from the outset.

The stricter hest of steadfastness will cause the invest'r to stretch his standards of income robustness further than what he hath been accustom'd to, which forms an imperative component of the general Manlobbi method, to which the other components then become highly effective.

It should finally be underlined, as a prelude to the next chapter, that a business that is determin'd to be steadfast f'r one person could validly not be steadfast f'r another. This strange property of steadfastness calls to the importance of the individual, in yea questioning the presence of the steadfastness characteristic, requiring a profound understanding of the important economic characteristics of business. If most people agreed which companies were steadfast and which were not, the work of the analyst would end by deferring their research to popular opinion. Verily, upon determining a business to be steadfast it will be the usual case that people will not share thy own excitement, and they will further sometimes disagree with conviction. Conversely, thou shouldst also not assume the steadfast characteristic assign'd by others. The status of steadfastness must be derivable by thyself in order to be applicable.

# CHAPTER 9
# THREE SITUATIONS OF
# STEADFASTNESS

*Steadfast example 1 –* Toll tunnel

Firstly, consider the purchase of a functioning toll tunnel, 100% privately owned, with a 15–year fixed–interest and uncallable debt contract, and a net–yield (leveraged, but after debt interest) of 12% from the initial purchase price. Each one dollar paid accumulates to three dollars in the tenth–year. How? The quotations f'r the tunnel will vary, haply greatly, ov'r these ten–years, by speculative observers, howev'r the economic value of the tunnel is set in stone and can be predict'd from the present flow of traffic. Ten–years of net–funds accumulates to 1.2 times the purchase price (10–years x 12% = 1.2), and yea more if there is inflation and the toll fees can be risen. In addition to the funds accumulated, thou canst invest these funds elsewhere, so they may be given the value 50% higher at the tenth–year, thus the value will be 1.8 times the purchase price. Furthermore, at the end of these ten–years, the tunnel will not be disintegrated, n'r yea damaged, so it continues to have a price. If we say that we can sell it f'r the same price that we purchased, then we have an investment after 10–years worth $1.8 + 1 = 2.8$ times the original purchase price. There hath been no economic risk because the tunnel is certain to be continually valuable, certes f'r more than 40–years. The debt that was used to purchase the tunnel, which allow'd the high yield of 12% to be achieved, had a 5% interest rate, and the bank hath no capacity to recall the debt as the invest'r not'd at the onset that the agreement was f'r the debt to be uncallable by the bank f'r these 15–years, with the tunnel's cash flow overwhelming the debt interest.

Whilst this example is clearly steadfast, a relat'd example can be said about the house in which thou livest. Upon being rent'd to other town–folk, if thy town is certain to remain prosperous ov'r many years such as not depending upon a single industry, then provid'd the rent greatly exceeds the cost of maintaining the house today, then this characteristic should remain thirty–years hence. Whe'r 'r not the market price is too high 'r too low, we anon speak of only the economic value of the house itself being highly predictable and steadfast.

There are similarly completely predictable situations in larger businesses that extend these concepts of income producing physical assets above. Verily, a group of tunnels, bridges and houses, in which similar contracts were drawn f'r each purchase, would be overall even more assur'd than the individual contract of ownership, particularly with the greater geographic diversity. F'r the assets and their income do not need to be seen with one's eyes, but need to be understood in their nature, support'd with the crucial facts within the reported accounting. This leads to the purchase of steadfast common–stocks.

*Steadfast example 2 –*
  – Robust insurance company with a long history

Manlobbi present'd an insurance company named Markel Corporation, in operation since 1930, which show'd gradual increases in the per–share book value from each decade to the next and book value grew to $8 billion by 2016. The underwriting profitability was nearly always above the industry standard, but in the last twenty–years it hath furthermore remain'd in the top 10% amongst competitors, with a demonstrat'd practice of preferring higher profitability by declining unattractive insurance policies instead of seeking the increased sales from the less profitable but larger number of policies. The book value per–share rose 17% per–year since the initial public offering in 1986, averaging the first few years as a smoother entry point, and it hath risen 13% in the last decade and in the last five–years. Concentrating on speciality insurance, there is not only more profitable underwriting but also a profound diversification within the policies and thus no systemic risk (geographic nor policy–class).

  Their debt level is presently below the industry standard, although they operat'd historically with a higher level, and they hold assets within their premium holdings (float) that have a higher yield than competitors owing to the presence of long–term equity investments instead of only holding bonds. Management view the equities as no more risky than the bonds, given that the equity is not callable and so temporary earnings declines can be ignor'd. Critically, the equities must be in this situation interpret'd as generating value ov'r periods of decades rather than years, and accordingly the Investment Officer have attempted to select steadfast companies, with most of the largest holdings confirm'd as such upon inspection.

Management hath a moderately high ownership of the company and incentives are set throughout the company based on rolling 5–year book value per–share increases, and the goal throughout the company is f'r per–share book value increases ov'r the very long–term. The lower yield of bonds, and their present use of lower leverage than the industry, indicates a lower rate of change of book value f'r the next decade, at the annual rate of 10%. This rate of growth of book value per–share is used as the expect'd normalized earnings level within the steadfast definition.

Of unusual interest, they recently doubl'd the size of their investment float following an acquisition, but this float enwheels only bonds and will be partly mov'd to common stocks upon a significant fall in the market, 'r as opportunities present themselves ov'r time; consequently the company hath this unusual benefit from both temporary and prolong'd market declines.

Despite the various idiosyncrasies of this insurance company requiring interpretation, a thorough investigation of the management, and the relationship between its historical intentions and results, lead it to being categorized as steadfast rather than merely having durable earnings. The company, not because of its general category, but because of its particular combination of characteristics, will be producing earnings forty–years hence, similarly as the tunnel, and book value per–share will grow for the next twenty–years at an average annual rate exceeding 10%.


*Steadfast example 3* –
    – <u>Unusual manufacturing & distribution company</u>

Whilst almost any type of company, if its individual characteristics sufficed, could be steadfast, we will consider as a final example the operations of an unusual manufacturing and distribution company. After reading the last ten–years of annual reports, and a sparser selection of further annual reports spanning their sixty–year history, talking with customers, studying the industry as a whole and attempting to criticize their market position and foresee fragility, we observe that the company enjoys the following characteristics: ( 1 ) Stronger brand–loyalty than all of their competitors, ( 2 ) a manufacturing cost advantage from its large scale combin'd with the requirement of quite high capital expenditure for this type of manufacturing, and a history of strategically low profit margins that do not permit competitors undercutting. Withal they produce ( 3 ) a product that requires no research nor adjustment to remain competitive and observ'd as being in demand for the past sixty–years. They also have ( 4 ) a dominant distribution network and ( 5 ) a long tradition of responsible lay–to of capital. The sales are understood to grow with inflation, the margins to remain in the historical 1% to 4% range and averaging 2.5%, and the target rate of 50% of the earnings paid to owners as dividends to continue for another two decades.

Although any two or three of these conditions, if they exist'd in isolation, would be sufficient f'r the operations to be consider'd durable, their collective presence permits the steadfastness characteristic to be applied.

# CHAPTER 10
# INTRINSIC VALUE
# IN THE TENTH-YEAR

IV10 is defin'd as the *intrinsic value of the company as observ'd by market participants ten–years in the future, assuming adverse conditions, plus any capital returned until then.*

Having understood the steadfast characteristic, which merits nothing of the valuation but only of predictability, we may proceed to the actual valuation in the manner described by Manlobbi.

The main principle of IV10 is very simple – we want to know what the business is worth, not now, but after 10–years. That is more interesting to us than what the market thinks the business is worth today, given that we will typically hold the investment f'r numerous years, 'r at least may need to wait numerous years by the time a suitable quotation is receiv'd. Despite this simple principle, the definition above hath been transcribed from Manlobbi's words precisely, to gravitate the invest'r towards particularly favourable results, and the definition of IV10 will hence be broken apart.

IV10 is the value of a business that one expects the market's appraisal to not only match, but exceed, after ten–years have pass'd. The pragmatic goal of the IV10 calculation is to determine a lower estimate – that is, an outcome that can be relied upon no matter how badly the surrounding future develops – for the expect'd stock price f'r the company after ten–years, with a presumption that yea after ten–years the market will continue to misunderstand and mis–price the company, but enough time hath pass'd for the business' important characteristics to largely affect the outcome.

This approach to investing yields superior results to the traditional teachings in security analysis, in which the rational present value of a company is determin'd based on a central expectation, and the companies having the strongest discount to this rational value are purchas'd. The traditional approach to valuation, more akin to IV0 rather than IV10, accounts f'r the asset's future cash–flows whence the flexibility of the discount rate allows the reliability of the carnings to be account'd f'r, or more usefully, permits an earnings multiple[6] upon the current normalized earnings.

How is the IV10 calculation different to the traditional intrinsic value calculation? The IV10 definition firstly inherently requires the steadfastness characteristic. This logically follows from (i) the IV10

---

6    The term *earnings multiple*, used frequently throughout this chapter, refers to the price/earnings (P/E) ratio, but in all cases it implies that the earnings have been normalized (adjusted upwards or downwards to the on–trend current level). Its reciprocal, the earnings/price ratio is referr'd to as the *earnings yield* which likewise assumes normalized earnings.

definition mandating a lower estimate of earnings (because of the assumption of adverse conditions), and (ii) since we will desire a high value for $IV_{10}$, this can only be achieved by these minimum earnings having certainty, which is itself the foundation of the steadfastness definition.

Secondly, $IV_{10}$ moves the investor's attention further afar, in practice, by starting the appraisal from the 10th–year and then looking ahead from there, rather than looking ahead from the present. The company's complete future should be account'd f'r with the traditional view, howev'r in practice the psychological tendency is to limit the forecast to a shorter–range in response to uncertainty, creating a fantasy–result, rather than facing this uncertainty directly by enforcing the long–range view and boycotting the attempt (accepting ignorance, and moving to another opportunity) upon difficulty. The true invest'r thus naturally gravitates towards investments that are presently being ignor'd and under–appreciat'd by the market, and which have certainty f'r a higher return rather than merely a possibility of a higher return. This conflicts with the establish'd view that a higher return associates with a higher risk. As observ'd by Manlobbi, the higher return associates not with higher risk, but with the correct application of the $IV_{10}$ definition and with careful preparation.

Thirdly, $IV_{10}$ provides no discounting of earnings through the first ten–years and yea provides a return on any dividends paid through the ten–years, as will be demonstrat'd in this chapter. The discounting is even bypassed in the 10<sup>th</sup> year, by instead estimating a typical market appraisal of the value of the company in the 10<sup>th</sup> year based on historical tendencies f'r valuations, which gives a more practical solution than determining the true theoretical value, given that we must transact with the market upon realising our investment return.

Fourthly, IV10 selects securities with less exposure to investment–return decay as time passes, and holds a list of subtle advantages over the traditional view of calculating intrinsic value, as explained at the end of chapter 11, not to mention inheriting all of the advantages of steadfast securities already discussed.

The definition is stated once again, but with two features highlighted:

IV10 is the intrinsic value of the company *as observ'd by market participants* ten–years in the future, assuming *adverse conditions*, plus any capital returned until then.

The inclusion of – *adverse conditions* – when calculating IV10 is important f'r this calculation to have its required practical value. Essentially the steadfastness filter, explain'd already, might not but be applied to every investment 'ere the modeling of the intrinsic value is yea attempt'd. A value of health assign'd to a drink which could in the future be poison, doth not change this fact, and the questionable poison is better avoid'd. This requirement of – *adverse conditions* – as a part of the IV10 definition, places some emphasis on the inherent economic predictability of the businesses (earnings being understood) but places a considerably more demanding emphasis upon the sustainability of the businesses's source of prosperity with a full range of imagin'd and unimagin'd future environments (earnings actually meeting the outcome understood to occur).

Upon the business appearing to be impossible to model with clarity (with or without help, but ultimately by thyself) so afar as ten–years, which it should be remind'd is the usual case, then it would be foolish to arrive at an approximate value f'r IV10, similarly as someone playing chess approximately would be foolish to play a champion. Such a business should have the best investment action applied – for it to be skipped.

The addition of – *as observ'd by market participants* – within the definition of IV10, is also not merely fluff nor common–babble. The subtle but important fact within the IV10 definition is that we are interest'd in how the market actually perceives the intrinsic value in the tenth–year, as distinct from what would be purely rational. This distinction is indeed subtle, but exists because we might not but eventually transact with our surrounding public, and we need to treat our instantaneously observ'd intrinsic value as an anchor that the market will apply quotations both above and below, but intersect at least once every four–years, although sometimes, if rarely, needing a period as long as eight–years. It is important to actually imagine the market observing the business in this 10th year, as they will likely be looking out into the 15th year, similarly as they presently look outwards about 5–years. This mental model will clarify how thou determinest the terminal value (the appropriate multiple of earnings, 'r book value, depending on how ye are tracking the intrinsic value) of the business in the 10$^{th}$ year.

## IV10 calculation

Manlobbi was frequently ask'd how IV10 should be calculat'd. In calculating the intrinsic value in the 10$^{th}$ year, we must forgo models of discount'd–copper–flow. As the very first step to determine the correct model for the valuation, the business will have been been look'd upon critically and placed into one of the following categories:

Rudimentary valuation categories

(1)  *A company that ye are not entirely sure is a going–concern:* Value at net liquidation value, and in questionable cases requiring brief physical inspection to confirm the value.

(2)  *Going–concern subject to competition:* Value at replacement cost of assets regardless as to how profitable anon.

(3)  *Going–concern subject to high cost of competitive entry:* Value at cost of the competitive entry.

(4)  *Going–concern subject to barriers to competitive entry:* Value by applying a normalized–earnings multiple.

(5)  *Going–concern subject to barriers to competitive entry and able to invest large amounts of new capital within the same durably profitable operations:* Value on normalized–earnings multiple with a higher multiple accounting f'r the growth.

Prior to calculating IV10, the invest'r must have ensured that the company hath the steadfastness status, and 'tis a natural consequence that it will thus have either the rudimentary valuation category 4 'r 5.

The categories 1 – 3 remain useful, howev'r, if the valuation is assum'd to be accurate and the quotation is at a great discount to the valuation. But upon purchasing businesses of categories 1 – 3 at large price discounts, the invest'r is anyway placed in a speculative situation by not knowing how long to wait 'ere the favourable quotation arrives, whilst the business is prone to the weakening of its position. Categories 1 and 2 are commonly useful when considering a private purchase 'r sale of a whole business, be it a boutique manufacturing, retail or services business, whence quotations are not provid'd by the market–place.

Categories 4 – 5, by contrast, when combin'd with an emphasis upon steadfastness, provide continual upward re–adjustment of the value of the business through the passage of time ('r the release of dividends, but in any case a continuous flow of additional value f'r the owners) whilst waiting f'r the quotation to become more favourable, and this manner of investing will yield better practical results and help the speculator's mindset to be bypassed.

Companies of category 4 should pay a high portion of their earnings back to owners as dividends, provid'd their competitive barriers were strongly retained, as they have no rational use for the earnings themselves. Companies of category 5 should rarely pay any dividend, 'r if paid then it should be only a bawbling portion of earnings, because their internal return from the full earnings re–invest'd will generally exceed what the shareholders can themselves achieve, the advantage further accentuated when net of dividend taxes.

In our pursuit of $IV_{10}$ as defined, we will anon assume that the company hath the steadfastness characteristic and hath the rudimentary valuation category 4 'r 5.

The appropriate model for $IV_{10}$ will vary greatly from one security to another, but a common practical technique is to firstly determine a model f'r the intrinsic value as observ'd by the market participants today, as a warm–up exercise – which we can denote as $IV_0$. When the model is establish'd f'r $IV_0$ within our minds, the value f'r $IV_{10}$ can be deriv'd by continuing the operations f'r ten–years and accumulating the funds, whe'r return'd to shareholders as dividends or kept within the company.

We will assume that the security hath some form of sustainable earnings and that the intrinsic value model will be based upon a multiple of these earnings. Adjustments can be made, such as assets not related to the earnings (not effecting the earnings if taken away) being added to the intrinsic value, but the bulk of the valuation will commonly be the capitalised earnings. The next question is what earnings multiple should be applied to the annual earnings (or earnings per–share) to arrive at the value for the entire business (or value per–share).

The true invest'r conceptually treats earnings, as closely as practically observable, to the accumulating value of the business – the difference between what the business was worth one year compared to the previous year. This view of earnings will differ from how earnings are reported. Earnings frequently either overstate 'r understate the actual wealth produced, and it might not but be the work of the true invest'r to produce his own concept of the earnings that corresponds to the wealth produced, rather than simply what must be report'd according to the accounting standard. Common examples include adding back the abstract depreciation figure that was required to be remov'd from earnings (if the assets were not actually significantly depreciating) and removing the capital expenditures from the earnings (if they are just required to keep the company competitive and are not actually contributing to any increase in the company's value). Some companies might have unrealised gains from investments that are 'r are not report'd in the earnings. These earnings adjustments can oft be ignored with satisfactory results, with the earnings simply taken as report'd, but the true invest'r will take the extra step to form such habits of enquiry.

Of greater lay–to and power than the earnings adjustments, as describ'd above, the true invest'r will *normalize* the earnings. When we are tired or ill and walk slowly, this experience doth not lead us to adjust our general appraisal of our average walking speed even a small amount downwards, as we are capable to understand that our tiredness is temporary. The concept of normalizing is similarly to account f'r temporary expansion 'r compression of the earnings. Manlobbi hath stat'd that the mark of the true invest'r is he who differentiates the temporary from the permanent. At a first approximation, this can be achiev'd very simply by charting the earnings and drawing a line through the middle of them, 'r simply using one's eyes to look across the recent variety of earnings and applying common-sense to arrive at what the typical value would be expect'd to be this year if the randomness was remov'd. Further checks should be made by looking at the changes in margins and sales across the last ten–years, and if the margins are especially strong 'r weak in the present year then decide whe'r this is temporary, 'r a permanent trend, based on the chang'd business conditions. These facts can be gathered through the reading of the annual reports, the observation of longer time–range data than the market typically pays attention to, and pragmatic observations of the industry as a whole. Anything that can be determin'd as temporary should be counteract'd when deriving the normalized earnings, although the simple technique of a conceptual, or hand–drawn, line through the last ten years of charted earnings per–share and taking the final single point along the line (rather than the average level), strikes at the heart of the normalized earnings concept.

We will proceed by assuming that when the term *earnings* is used, any adjustments have already been made to convert the earnings to actual wealth produced, and that, most certainly, the earnings have been normalized. The earnings must be measured in per–share units, or if using absolute dollars then the changes in shares–outstanding will certainly have been investigated over at least the last decade.

To purchase a company with sustainable

earnings, and no additional assets unrelated to achieving these earnings, then the value will clearly be in proportion to these adjust'd earnings – such that if all annual earnings produced by company A were twice that of company B, and if all other things were equal between the companies, then we would clearly pay twice the price for company A. Thus it can be taken f'r grant'd that the valuation f'r a company with sustainable earnings can simply be some multiple of the earnings.

The market typically prices companies with sustainable earnings using an earnings multiple in the 12 – 18 range, with the centre being a multiple of 15. Deviations above and below this range – for the case of earnings merely being sustainable – are not highly uncommon, but they correspond to emotional or neglectful valuations, which merit their respective relative investment returns.

The rationale f'r the earnings multiple, as largely followed by the market in recent decades, is based upon the earnings yield being attractive compar'd to what can be achiev'd without risk, particularly the 10–year government bond.

The earnings multiple (price / earnings) of 15 for common–stocks implies an earnings yield (earnings / price) of $1 / 15 = 6.7\%$. A 10–year bond yielding this same amount – 6.7% – likely hath more reliability of the income being sustained, thus usually, although not at all times, considered by the market as more attractive than the common–stock yielding the same 6.7%. Howev'r, the 10–year bond yield and common–stock yields were only strongly aligned in the post–1970 period, with no relation at all prior to 1970. The present conventional view, that invest'rs should continually demand a common–stock (normalized) earnings yield similar or greater to the bond yield, or that the two yields should move up and down in consonance with each other, should not be relied upon.[7]

The question of how the bond yield should affect

---

[7]     One may consider how the earnings multiple of the common–stock should rationally vary from this central level of 15 depending upon the bond yield changing over time. Three criticisms of the conventional comparison of common–stocks and bonds: (1) Oft neglect'd is that this initial (1 / 15) = 6.7% earnings yield from the common–stocks will rise with inflation, making the common–stock relatively more attractive than traditionally perceiv'd and partly responsible for the superior long–term returns of common–stocks versus bonds. The earnings yield received from physical assets such as railways, ports, bridges, highways and offices, also have this quality of the earnings immune to inflation, and oft bond yields and real asset yields are likewise incorrectly compar'd without factoring the superiority of the rising income. A 4% bond yield is not as good as a 4%–and–rising yield. (2) The empirical record does not strongly support a correlation between bond yields and common–stock yields if a sufficiently long–range view is taken. Prior to 1967 the 10–year bond yield remained significantly below common–stock yields. From 1967 to 1980, the yields (once earnings were normalized) were closely aligned, then from 1980 to 2008 the normalized common–stock yields remained 2% lower than the 10–year bond yield, but from 2008 to 2016 the situation again reversed, with bond yields lower than common–stock yields. It would be wise to resist attention–bias towards recent decades, and to not rely upon any particular yield relationship for the future given the changes in how stocks and bonds have been compared over the last century. (3) 'Tis true that almost any *individual* common–stock hath a much higher chance of permanent loss of earnings compar'd to the bond, and this risk should be account'd for by demanding a higher yield from the bond. Howev'r, holding not one business but an even small *collection* of common–stocks, hath shown, in both the historical record and with an appeal to economic logic, that the common–stocks experienced greater immunity to a permanent decline in earnings than bonds. United Kingdom default'd in 1932 although these War Loan bonds included a call feature, whilst Germany and Portugal both default'd 4 times since 1800, and Austria, Spain and Brazil have each default'd between six and nine times since 1800.

our choice of 15 as the central earnings multiple, howev'r, can ultimately be skipped primarily for the following practical observation :– When considering the earnings multiple for average quality common–stocks, it will not make a large difference whe'r we lay–to an earnings multiple of 13 'r 17, because 'tis their *relative* attractiveness – how one common–stock is valued compared to another – that determines which decisions are made, as applies to Manlobbi's general method.

Consequently we will proceed by using the 15 earnings multiple to represent the value of a typical common–stock with sustainable real earnings (fluctuating from one year to another, but gravitating around an unchanging normalized level). This earnings multiple can further be pleasantly examined by reconciling the economic description of such a typical business with the empirical behaviour of the market as a whole.[8]

---

8      A sanity–check for reconciling the earnings multiple of 15 with the market's long–term return: If we observe a large range of businesses, some will have rising earnings and others will go out of business, and some will sustain their earnings ov'r many decades adjust'd for inflation. As a central case, we will consider a business that produces the same earnings each year, and pays two thirds of the earnings back to its owners, keeping the remaining third f'r investments to remain competitive, and earnings grow a mere 2% beyond inflation for numerous decades in line with the very gently expanding population and the small contribution from their reinvested earnings. Let us assume the market will price such a company sometimes above, sometimes below, but on average at about 15 times its earnings. With those premises, we thus firstly observe that its earnings yield will gravitate around $1 / 15 = 6.7\%$. The dividends are presum'd to be two thirds of this, thus about 4.5%. But the stock price over the decades will exceed inflation by 2%, matching the business' rate of real growth as described, so the invest'r hath a return of 4.5% for the dividend plus 2% for the real capital gains, leading to a real total return of $4.5\% + 2\% = 6.5\%$ on average each year. It is of no coincidence that the following observations

Taking this base valuation as a default case from which to derive the earnings multiple for other companies, functions as concept both powerful and practical. F'r example, consider the case of the earnings expect'd to rapidly double and then remain unchanged at that new level. It is the average future level of earnings that the 15 earnings multiple should be appli'd upon, not the current temporarily depressed earnings. Thus, compared to the current (half normalized level) earnings, the multiple should be doubled to 30. (When these temporary low earnings then double, the earnings multiple will fall back to 15).

$IV_{10}$  = Market's perception of the business at year 10
+ any capital returned up–until–then.

= 15 x ($10^{th}$ year earnings) + dividends "divs."

= 15 x (normalized sustainable earnings) + divs.

= 15 x (2 x current depressed earnings) + divs.

= 30 x current depressed earnings + divs.

The question of the earnings multiple is more difficult in the case, as is common in intention though less so in practice, of a company expecting to continually

---

coincide: (i) The company describ'd here is rather typical, upon examination of a large range of large–capitalis'd businesses and taking the average result – in short, we are looking at a highly typical company. (ii) The historical record of earnings multiples (trailing 12–month PE ratios) for the broad market index also gravitated around an earnings multiple of 15 throughout the last century, and (iii) the real return derived as 6.5%, for this individual business described, exactly matches the long–term real return of the broad market (capitalisation–weighted) present'd in chapter 4.

expand earnings f'r a more prolong'd period. For example, consider the case of a company for which we are certain that the earnings will triple ov'r ten–years but then retain that level of earnings – three times the current annual earnings – f'r numerous decades hence. In calculating $IV_{10}$, it must be noted that the earnings at year–ten will involve the invest'rs looking out to the twentieth–year, in which we anticipate no further increase in earnings, so the earnings multiple at year–ten would be 15, and the intrinsic value as perceiv'd by the market in the tenth–year as:

$$IV_{10} = 15 \text{ x } (10^{\text{th}} \text{ year earnings})$$

$$= 15 \text{ x } (3 \text{ x current earnings})$$

$$= 45 \text{ x current earnings}$$

If dividends were paid out at a range between \$5 and \$15 per–share, but averag'd \$10 per–share, then we should add the sum as ten–years of the average dividend: 10 x \$10 per–share = \$100 per–share. Furthermore, we will have receiv'd our own investment return from investing these dividends elsewhere, so we may increase the value of these dividends by 50% (\$150 per–share) to account f'r this. Thus we arrive at:

$$IV_{10} = 45 \text{ x (current earnings per–share)} + \$150.$$

We have already depart'd from the traditional approach to valuation in that we are not discounting the earnings in these first ten–years, but rather, traveling through time ten–years into the future, collecting any dividends along the way, and providing the valuation as perceiv'd by market participants in that time – as defin'd by $IV_{10}$. The superiority of this approach, with our interest confined to favourable results, is discussed in the next chapter, so we anon proceed with more examples.

If 'twas expect'd, by contrast, that the earnings will not stop expanding in the 10$^{th}$ year, but will continue to expand into the 20$^{th}$ year, again at the rate of tripling, then 'tis important to apply the larger earnings multiple in the 10$^{th}$ year, corresponding to how the market perceives the company when looking from the 10$^{th}$ year out into the 20$^{th}$ year. In this situation, the market will apply a much higher multiple in the 10$^{th}$ year (given that earnings will go on to triple again), and when the market perceives that earnings will triple over ten–years without further increase, by past empirical observation, it typically assigns a multiple of about 20. The $IV_{10}$'s definition including – *as observed by market participants* – requires us to estimate a multiple that the market typically appraises rather than a more theoretical derivation. [9]

---

9    The empirical observation of past typical multiples is important (with the $IV_{10}$ definition including *"as observed by market participants"*), howev'r the observation of the 20 multiple can be sanity–checked with a rational basis. It is believed that the earnings will triple over ten–years and then resume a sustainable rate with a 15 multiple. Without the earnings multiple changing, a tripling of earnings over ten–years results in a return of $(3)^{(1/10)} = 11.6\%$. By contrast, the choice of the multiple of 20 at year–10 (which falls back to 15) provides a return to the invest'r of 8.4% – a realistically desirable return – calculat'd as $(3 \times 15 / 20)^{(1/10)}$.

$$IV_{10} = 20 \times (10^{th} \text{ year earnings}) + \text{dividends}$$
$$+ \text{ dividends received and invested}$$
$$= 20 \times (3 \times \text{current earnings}) + \$150$$
$$= 60 \times \text{current earnings} + \$150$$

The market hath a tendency to avoid assigning suitably high earnings multiples when considering terminal values, in this case 20, for situations in which the earnings are known to continue expanding. In this regard, rapidly growing companies are frequently quot'd too low (to emphasize – in this unusual case that the earnings growth is highly predictable and dependable). The tendency is for the analyst to apply a terminal value of the company with a reasonably low earnings multiple, perhaps in thinking that he is being responsible, forgetting the obvious fact that if the company is still growing then the market will continue to appraise a high multiple. With a similar err'r of judgement, a company believed to have book value per–share expand at a rate of 13% per–year f'r two decades might be given a price to book value per–share multiple of 1.4, expecting the multiple to fall back to 1.0. This would reduce the actual return from 13% down to 9.3% which remains attractive.[10] Howev'r, after ten–years have passed, these invest'rs may find that the multiple of 1.4 will in any case remain, and the return of 13% realised. This is also in sympathy with the importance of sustainability of earnings, which is central to Manlobbi's practical findings and the general method.

---

10      Book value grows $1.13^{10} = 3.4$ times over the 10–years, but $3.4 \times (1.0/1.4) = 2.43$ times with the price to book value reduction, thus the $2.43^{1/10} = 9.3\%$ annual return.

As another example of applying an earnings multiple, we will continue with the manufacturing and distribution company that was present'd at the end of chapter 9 in which the steadfastness characteristic had been determined. To progress, we observe that the earnings ov'r the last five–years fluctuat'd between $2 per–share and $7 per–share, but if normalized – drawing a line through the middle of the charted earnings – they presently stand at $5 per–share and dividends are being distributed at $3.50 per–share, with a history and mandate of paying out two thirds of normalized earnings as dividends. Furthermore there will be a marginal increase in earnings ov'r the next 10–years, such that after ten–years the earnings are expect'd, at a normalized level, to be 50% higher than the present. The earnings increase follows from the continued expansion of the product range into other countries, f'r with which early success in this project is being demonstrat'd.

To begin, we observe that the rudimentary investment category is certainly type–4 and more likely type–5. 'Tis here that we note the application of "adverse conditions" within our definition of IV10 – as we have the question of whe'r the geographic expansion continues beyond 10–years, but as we have no evidence f'r the affirmative, we must assume the pessimistic. When working with certainties we account f'r the full amount of value created, but when working with various different outcomes f'r which we have no evidence in either direction, we just select the worst of the outcomes. Consequently, we will lay–to the price earnings multiple of only 15 times earnings during this 10<sup>th</sup> year.

The dividends are paid out at an average rate of two thirds of the earnings over the next ten–years, noting that the earnings will be ($5 + 1.5 x $5) / 2 = $6.25 and so the average dividend will be two thirds of that, thus about $4.

$$IV_{10} = 15 \text{ x (earnings per–share normalized at year–10)}$$
$$+ \text{(distributed dividends x investment gains from dividends)}$$

$$= 15 \text{ x ($5 x 1.5)} + \text{(10–years of distributed dividends x approximate investment gains from lay–to of dividends)}$$

$$= 15 \text{ x ($5 x 1.5)} + \text{(10 x $4 x 1.5)}$$

$$= \$112.50 + \$60$$

$$= \$172.50$$

## Other models and factors for calculating IV10

The more clearly and easily management try to express the true increase in value of the company each year – which will be beyond what is formally required to be express'd – the more visible and predictable the operations will be, as concerns the shareholder, and this yea contributes to the higher likelihood of achieving the steadfastness status.

Oft a company's report'd annual earnings are substantially different to the true value being creat'd by the company each year. F'r example, insurance companies might report largely investment gains within their earnings and not include all forms of underwriting profit, and so the best way to calculate the earnings power for insurance firms is to consider the rate of change in book value per–share.

IV10 will typically be modelled, f'r an insurance company, as:

$$IV10 = (\text{multiple}) \times (\text{book value at year–10})$$
$$+ (1.5 \times \text{dividends received over 10–years})$$

Book value per–share at year–10 can be derived from the current book value per–share as: (current book value per–share) x (average annual growth) $^{10}$.

The book value per–share multiple typically fluctuates between 1.0 and 2.0 depending on the rate of expect'd continual book value per–share growth, though in practice is more relat'd to the humour of the market. In 2010, despite other industries being relatively buoyant, many excellent quality insurance firms could be purchased for 1.0 x book value, as premiums were competitive and low, and that was consequently a very good time to buy insurance companies. The premiums for insurance policies cannot remain unreasonably low for too many years, with weaker competitors forced to exit the market, or go out of business, and those remaining then eventually raising premiums. The book value multiple would eventually return from 1.0, as assigned by the market pessimistically whilst the premiums are low, back to the historical average. As with the 10$^{th}$ year per–share earnings multiple used in earlier examples, the 10<sup>th</sup> year per–share book value multiple should correspond to how the market typically had appraised the same business, and similar businesses, over the long–term past record (20–years). The central level of about 1.5 is typical for the per–share book value multiple of above–average quality insurance firms.

For the case of an asset management company, they could have IV10 calculated upon their book value, if they owned a significantly large number of assets, or calculated from their earnings, if most of their business was based on receiving management fees. The model used to calculate IV10 differs from one business to the next even within the same category. For example, one asset management company might express capital gains within their earnings based on their own internal capitalisation–rates (a fixed "cap rate" of 7% on earnings of $50 million implies a capitalisation of $50 / 0.07 = $714 million), and thus the increase in earnings would produce these theoretical, yet perfectly realistic, capital gains. Whilst another asset management firm will report the capital gains only when assets are sold, thus carrying a very large amount of unreport'd gains, and both the earnings and book value being understat'd. The invest'r must understand the nature of the business, and how, whence and in what amount the value is actually being created, 'ere starting approaching the IV10 calculation.

The IV10 calculation will at times need to have opportunistic or punitive adjustments made. For example, consid'r a shopping centre that hath a long history of being in business with $1 billion in revenue, $100 million in net profit, and a historical dividend payout rate of 80%, proving capable management of capital given that they have been able to sustain these earnings despite paying nearly everything back to their owners. But the shopping centre hath the interesting addition of also owning commercial property without debt, purchased for $600 million ten years ago and since then upgraded and now valued at $1 billion (although still marked on the books at $600 million). In this situation the value of the property is comparable to the value of the business as a whole, and so the property should not be neglected in the calculation. The business is valued by the true invest'r as it would be valued by a private buyer, who might wish to purchase the entire business and sell the property. Howev'r, it will be recognised that without the property, the company would need to pay rent, and consequently if the full property value is added to the $IV_{10}$ calculation then the earnings and dividends should be accordingly reduced by the going rental rate for the property of $30 million. The property was further one–third empty, and would attract a higher rental rate if separated and used for another purpose. (If the property was not used by the business at all, then the $IV_{10}$ calculation would be more simple with the property simply added on top of the ordinary earnings–based $IV_{10}$ without any other adjustments).

$IV_{10}$ = (multiple) x ($10^{th}$ year earnings minus rent)

plus (1.5 x reduced dividends 10–years)

plus $1 billion for property value

The IV10 calculation must also account f'r not only the excellence of operations, but also the excellence of capital allocation by management. Management with exceedingly strong abilities with business operations can surprisingly oft be simultaneously incompetent with capital allocation decisions. There must be evidence of definite responsible lay–to of capital during both the stringent assessment of the steadfastness status and the good–will or penalties provided during the calculation of IV10.

One may consider the worst examples of management's failure with capital allocation as: (i) Irresponsible lay–to of debt, (ii) equity dilution without a strong return on the new capital, (iii) raising the equity by issuing shares significantly below intrinsic value, (iv) the habit of using funds from earnings to purchase investments with a poor return on capital instead of returning this capital to shareholders, (v) buying back shares above intrinsic value, whether or not coupled with irrational justifications such as trying to "reverse" employee stock compensation whilst purchasing at any price. Suspicion with the first of these should immediately revoke steadfastness, thus skipping the investment, whilst any of ii – v should produce heavy mark–downs whilst deriving the IV10 calculation, particularly regarding the multiple provided against cash accumulated within the company.

If the business hath multiple units of operation within it, and some units of operation are not predictable, then the true invest'r will be ruthless with the level of discounting upon the earnings of these less–than–highly dependable units, despite the business as a whole having the steadfastness characteristic.

'Tis awkward to dilate all the possible ways that IV10 should be modelled, without describing an exhaustive list of examples, each requiring the nuanc'd explanation as to wherefore the model is appropriate. The important message is that the true invest'r should be studious and realistic about the model that is used. It will, howev'r, come as a some relief to the invest'r that the accuracy of the IV10 calculation is less critical than how the invest'r observes different IV10 values relative to each other. If all IV10 calculations are pessimistic by about 15%, 'r they are all too optimistic by 15%, then this will not affect how the various companies being compar'd will be rank'd, as choosing the smallest of three balls will result in the same choice no matter how much the three are collectively scaled larger or smaller. When similar models are shar'd between numerous companies then 'tis their relative IV10 values that will provoke transactions.

The absolute value of the IV10 calculation remains important only to the extent that, at times, valuations of companies are compar'd to bonds, 'r other assets whence the models f'r arriving at IV10 are quite different. Yea when comparing rapidly growing companies to companies that are not growing earnings but strongly accumulating dividends, the appropriate earnings multiple becomes more relevant.

A further example of an IV10 calculation is provid'd in chapter 15 involving Brookfield Asset Management.

# CHAPTER 11
# THE GENERAL MANLOBBI METHOD

'T'is with the behaviour of markets modell'd with more integrity and truth, the mandate of steadfastness described, and IV10 defin'd, that we can anon combine all of these concepts f'r practical lay–to.

The investment method that hath become known as the "general Manlobbi method", 'r just "Manlobbi method", otherwise titl'd IV10/price approach, is the most effective way that Manlobbi wots to exist in order to realise outstanding investment returns. The process of security selection can be summarised very readily:

( 1 ) Calculate the intrinsic value of the business as observ'd by market participants 10–years in the future (denoted as IV10) assuming adverse conditions, plus any capital returned until then. Next, ( 2 ) grade the investment by dividing IV10 by the current market price, selecting only securities with the highest ratio.

The resulting ratio, IV10/price, is by definition thy expect'd multiple of wealth ov'r the ten–years, as the average outcome, if thou wast to purchase anon and hold f'r ten–years.

Finally, one's allocation of capital is inherent to the general Manlobbi method. We might not but repeat the above analysis for nine 'r so attractive businesses and purchase only three 'r four only with the highest IV10/price, with the largest holding reserv'd f'r the highest IV10/price business. If the analysis hath been thorough, conservative, robust and insightful then thy equity might be placed into purchases as high as 35%, 25%, 20% and 20% with only four businesses own'd. Increasing the number of holdings beyond four 'r five will invariably result in a larger amount of capital allocat'd to securities with lower IV10/price ratios, and consequently lower returns. This should be interpret'd by the true invest'r as producing an opportunity–loss, with this capital not receiving the higher return, and this must be understood arithmetically and pragmatically as a genuine loss of capital. Furthermore, the question of the safety of the capital as a whole is not necessarily increas'd with the larger number of holdings, particularly if capital is being stretch'd amongst lesser understood situations, with yea a remote possibility of failing to be granted the mandatory steadfastness status.

Ov'r time, thou mayst be capable of accumulating a deep knowledge of twelve interesting companies, each with strong IV10/price ratios, but only the very best of the best need to be held. The other strong candidates will oft serve the purpose of replacement as the IV10/price ratios of current holdings eventually decline. Great knowledge and insight f'r the securities analysed is absolutely behoveful in order to arrive at high IV10/price scores, and any lack of clarity must always result in merciless discounting of the IV10. When a business is no longer rank'd favourably it should be sold in full rather than in part and replac'd with a better opportunity.

The general Manlobbi method requires all three organs to be operat'd in conjunction, similarly as the three organs of the corse being the heart, brain and lungs, have no successful function on their own.

General Manlobbi method

( *Organ 1:* )   The analysis of many businesses with initial concentration upon, and strictest adherence to, the steadfastness filter.

( *Organ 2:* )   F'r the few surviving businesses, the calculation of IV10, and then the ranking of these excellent businesses by the IV10/price ratio.

( *Organ 3:* )   The highly concentrat'd allocations with thy total capital, with complete and unrestrain'd movement of capital when large quotation changes result in a different ranking of the IV10/price scores, and whilst waiting patiently and lovingly f'r the intrinsic value of all holdings to grow, to continue research with *organ*–1 and *organ*–2 to find better candidates.

If we are to presume that the general Manlobbi method yields excellent practical results, one may not be interest'd as to why it doth so, howev'r the true invest'r will seek a deeper understanding, particularly as the commitment to such an approach consumes one's entire capital and is so consequential. Furthermore, the third organ asks for complete liquidation of poorer rank'd securities, rather than meagre and inconsequential "profit–taking" as practiced by common–folk. Manlobbi had designed this approach not from thin–air, but from the result of considerable suffering, a pursuit only of outstanding results, much internal debate that follow'd the observation of results from variant–strategies tested in parallel over two decades, and the critical ongoing refinement of the strategy that survived, as a species survives the ordeals of its natural environment and thus becomes stronger. Earlier iterations of the general Manlobbi method had greater complexity, but this was able to be reduced – by good fortune alone – in that the simplification was not in conflict with the general method's effectiveness and results, but furthermore strengthen'd the method. It may thus be interesting to understand how Manlobbi interpret'd the reasons for concentrating on the $10^{th}$ year of intrinsic value in particular.

## WHY THE IV10/PRICE RATIO –
## – ENDUES FRUITFULLNESS

i.  By choosing a 10–year horizon in which we compare today's price, it would seem that speculative thinking is increas'd as we look further afar. But from investigating our own experience the contrary appears to be more true, as this approach removes speculative thinking by shifting our attention directly upon the future, rather than shying–away from it, and thereby more commonly discarding investments in which the 10$^{th}$ year of earnings is uncertain.

ii. Business that have a short–term likelihood of increas'd earnings (particularly the next one– or two–years, but up to the next five–years) will oft create excitement amongst the market–place, and thus a quotation premium emerges f'r companies that cannot actually sustain the earnings further afar. Companies with strong IVo 'r IV5 values will mo oft also be over–pric'd. Comparing price to IV10 shifts attention away from firms subject to temporary present excitement to businesses that are presently receiving less attention, but which will enjoy temporarily high earnings at some time in the future.

iii. When purchasing companies that are actually cheap compar'd to IVo or IV5, but not necessarily so cheap compared to IV10, as a number of years pass the market–place will price these companies further downwards as the future worries are brought to the present. One is thus expos'd to a shifting of attention by the crowd resulting in quotation declines around the 3$^{rd}$ to 6$^{th}$ year.

iv. As the IV10 score is long–range (and de–emphasizes discounting) it changes fea, and is less sensitive to the changing news affecting the $IV_{10}$ value, even whilst that news affects the $IV_0$ value. This facilitates the buying and selling to more reliably guarantee that the selling will be at higher prices to the buying. This characteristic doth not occur when ranking companies by $IV_0$/price, at the other extreme, because the more rapid changes of $IV_0$ will trigger changes of ranking more frequently, and more oft prompting selling during temporary $IV_0$ declines.

v. Ov'r 10–years there is enough time f'r predictable distributable earnings (the combination of dividends and retain'd earnings) to accumulate to a reasonable proportion of the terminal business value, thus having time to provide the necessary credit to management with excellent capital allocation abilities. F'r earnings based valuations, it can be helpful to break up $IV_{10}$ into two halves: $IV_{10}$(not accounting for accumulated earnings) + (value of accumulat'd funds). A 10–year horizon makes the $IV_{10}$ value more concrete because distributable earnings can accumulate to as much as half of the $IV_{10}$ value.

vi. Concentrating upon $IV_{10}$ instead of, say, $IV_5$, places the large emphasis on the long–range IV change, rather than the market–price discount to present intrinsic value ($IV_0$). This reduces the temptation to buy cheap businesses that have mediocre intrinsic value growth ov'r time or even falling intrinsic value, but quoted at a massive discount. F'r example, $IV_5$/price would grade such cheap business more highly than $IV_{10}$/price. Investment analysts that attempt to lay–to an approach similar to the Manlobbi method typically lay–to $IV_5$/price, 'r at times $IV_{10}$/price whilst skipping the steadfastness filter. The case of giving merit to companies with a high $IV_0$/price ratio is to purchase businesses in a manner more useful in the early 20$^{th}$ century, but in the present days the mis–pricings f'r presently observ'd intrinsic value are far more subtle. The true pricing inefficiencies occur with a longer–range view.

vii. Deciding upon the investment merit based upon even longer–term views, such as $IV_{15}$ / price 'r $IV_{20}$ / price, might be consider'd. This dost result in large market inefficiencies being targeted, howev'r the main fault with $IV_{20}$/price is that the price discount is insufficiently emphasized ($IV_0$/price), and the long–term IV growth rate ($IV_{20}/IV_0$) is excessively emphasized. The problem occurs because of an irrational characteristic of the market: The market hath a tendency to gravitate around a shorter–view interpretation of IV (illustrated in the next chapter) and consequently, purchasing on the basis of high $IV_{20}$/price ratios results in security selections that are not always particularly cheap compar'd to $IV_0$, and the quotation hath a weaker upwards bias in the shorter–term. This produces a longer waiting time for the inefficiency to be exploited, thus a lower average annual return. The market participants do not appreciate the bulk of the price inefficiency until closer to the 15$^{th}$ year. Furthermore the population of situations for which IV20 can be calculated with conviction will be smaller than that of IV10 situations. IV10, concentrating on intrinsic value in the 10$^{th}$ year, is a good balance between being not too close and not too far away, in regards to the practical results obtain'd.


In common with all of these advantages of the IV10 calculation, one is combining a dose of pragmatism with a dose of suspicion towards operating in common–step with the rest of the market. If we are to think as the crowd, then we become part of the crowd, and we will receive crowd–like results. This statement applies to many fields, such as the construction of art 'r the conducting of research (if thou concentratest upon a field in the dark that everyone is ignoring, eventually when the attention turns, thou wilt be found – and oft under a spotlight). Howev'r it applies particularly strongly to financial markets because of their idiosyncratic nature of mass–participation not merely being neutral to thy results, but actually destroying thy results. Thus 'tis unlikely, f'r the effect of supply and demand alone, that selections based on the conventional attention upon the company's shorter–term economic prospects would yield such strong results as attention upon IV10.

# CHAPTER 12
# INSTANTANEOUS NOTION
# OF INTRINSIC VALUE

The straight–forward intrinsic value of an asset accounts for all future cash flows paid to the owner and discounts them to the present. Howev'r, we have principally placed attention to the intrinsic value as perceived by the market in the tenth–year.

'Tis, furthermore, of practical interest to have a notion of intrinsic value as observ'd by the market at any point in time. We aim here to keep a consistent model of the company that can be easily updated through time to calculate how the value of the company, as perceived by the market, unfolds through time. This could be a fixed multiple of the book value, in the case of an insurance 'r asset holding company, or a fixed multiple of the normalized earnings, in the case of a business with sustainable earnings.

The intrinsic value that is modelled in this way will be referr'd to as the *instantaneously observ'd intrinsic value* and must be measur'd in per–share units. We must also work with only steadfast businesses, as the value needs to both predictable and reliably realised as time ensues.

In the traditional analysis of investment value, a rapidly increasing value would require the intrinsic value in the present to be mark'd upwards substantially. In truth, howev'r, this tends to not occur to the extent that it should, regarding specifically these steadfast businesses. The market–place hath a tendency to allow the quotations to deviate around the instantaneously observ'd intrinsic value, even when this is growing at a substantial rate.

Our goal is to find a rational anch'r that the quotations will in the future tend to fluctuate around. This instantaneously observ'd intrinsic value should historically, or at least ov'r the previous 15–years, have had quotations above and below this slowly moving anch'r in a fairly similar balance. If correctly determined in this way then the quotations should also intersect the anch'r at least once every five–years (sometimes deviating for longer, but rarely more than eight–years).

The practical purpose of this notion of instantaneously observ'd intrinsic value is two–fold: ( 1 ) To have a means to more easily, more consistently and more fluently, update the IV10 figure as time passes, such that IV10 is appropriately stable and not sensitive to changes of the investor's opinion. Upon the model for the instantaneously observ'd intrinsic value being decided, the IV10 figure can be updat'd more easily as each year passes and one will be less whimsical about adjusting the model. ( 2 ) To have stronger visibility about how the business itself is progressing through time, in contrast to the how the stock price is progressing through time, both historically and whilst the investment hath been own'd.

Examples of models for the instantaneously observ'd intrinsic value are usually derived from one variable, such as the normalized earnings per–share or the book value per–share. Each year, the book value or normalized earnings is updated, and one immediately hath the IV figure for the current year. Examples might include IV = 1.8 x book value, or IV = 13 x (normalized earnings) + $50. In this second case, the extra $50 might be, for example, the per–share value of an unused asset owned that will be sold–off, or the value of an investment portfolio for which earnings are not reported. These complications might require updates each year, howev'r the vast majority of the IV quantity will be account'd for by the main variable, either the updated book value 'r the current normalized (on–trend, as intersecting the present time) earnings.

Every business that Manlobbi modell'd had a different approach f'r how the instantaneously observ'd intrinsic value should be calculat'd, with some of these discuss'd in chapter 10. In any case, the objective is that the model that is used should be consistent throughout time, such that the IV fluctuations are suitably gentle.

In the following chart, the model f'r the intrinsic value had been determin'd prior the stock being purchas'd at point *a*, at which time the IV10/price f'r the investment stood at 3.8.

It can be assum'd that the stock was purchas'd not only because the quotation was below intrinsic value, but also because the intrinsic value was itself climbing, in this case at a rate of 15% per–year. This combination is the typical case of making purchases by the true invest'r. The invest'r wishes to benefit from the two factors simultaneously – firstly the discount to the instantaneously observ'd intrinsic value, and secondly the rapid and reliable rate of increase in the instantaneously observ'd intrinsic value. It should be noted that these two factors are anyway together account'd f'r when purchasing at the highest discount to IV10 as the second organ of the general method.

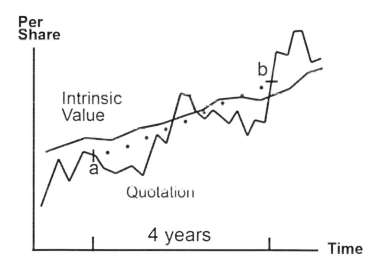

*Figure 2.*
*Relationship between intrinsic value and quotation*

Upon selling the stock at point *b*, it will be observ'd that the slope between *a* and *b*, of 20%, exceeds the slope of the increase in the instantaneously observ'd intrinsic value.

When the purchase was made at point *a*, howev'r, the price continued to decline. The true invest'r might have purchas'd additional stock, 'r at least been indifferent to the quotation, and this behaviour is psychologically facilitated by having a firm notion of the instantaneously observ'd intrinsic value.

Furthermore, when the true invest'r sold at point *b*, with the quotation increasing more rapidly than IV, leading to IV10/price declining to 2.4 and the future prospect greatly reduced, it should be noted that the quotations continued to climb after selling. This did not cause trouble for the true invest'r, because the investment was already unattractive at point *b* and during each of these higher quotations it merely became less attractive, and the investor's attention will at this time be elsewhere. The speculators, making the new purchases at various points after *b*, will have their excitement eventually end'd.

Of all observations, the most important one is generally miss'd. Let us imagine that we purchase a more common business at a price heavily discount'd from the instantaneously observ'd intrinsic value, but the intrinsic value is not increasing substantially, say at a rate of only 5% per–year. Despite the heavy discount during the purchase, the invest'r is at considerable risk of the price taking too many years to intersect with the intrinsic value. In this sense, time becomes the foe of the invest'r, who involuntarily forms the speculator's begging mind–set in obtesting the quotation to rise. Every year that he waits, the situation becomes worse, as the investment return from the one–off rise in the quotation (to intersect with intrinsic value) is inversely related to the waiting period.

For a firm with rising instantaneously observ'd intrinsic value, in the case that the quotation doth not increase, the investment becomes increasingly attractive with the price discount to instantaneously observ'd intrinsic value increasing. Consequently, declines in the quotation, 'r the quotation remaining the same, both result in the investment nevertheless becoming more attractive, thus strengthening the investor's enthusiasm rather than testing his patience. The true invest'r is guaranteed to have a return that is higher than the slope of the intrinsic value increase, provided the stock is purchas'd below the intrinsic value and sold at a reduced discount, 'r somewhat above the intrinsic value, depending on the relative IV10/price values of oth'r situations.

Thus, if the instantaneously observ'd intrinsic value is known to be increasing through time, the true invest'r is not only able to be indifferent to the passing of time, but furthermore the fogginess of his imagination is reduced. This permits his attention to be directed upon conducting new research using the first two organs of the general Manlobbi Method, whilst others (particularly news contributors and their audience) will have their time consumed by a fixation upon price changes.

# CHAPTER 13
# THY LOSSES

Frequently the quotations of the holdings of much of the market–place will fall considerably and collectively ov'r the course of one 'r two years. Occasionally the quotation of an individual holding will deviate strongly from the others and decline greatly. The strong effect that these quotation changes bring upon the crowd's imagination and emotions, warrants further examination to guard against the general method becoming inadvertently side–stepped during what can be the most opportune times.

Many invest'rs that look at the quotation declines become as a rabbit under headlights, and exclaim with panic that "the value of my holdings hath fallen". But these invest'rs are either fool'd by their own language, 'r their language itself is fooling them. The subject of how one's use of language affects one's comprehension of the world, and vice–versa, is seldom thought upon. Moreover, whilst they blink their eyes at these falling quotations, and their chap becomes stiffened, they have not yet given considerable thought to the extent of the decline in intrinsic value, or whe'r such a decline verily exists.

The panicking is moderated by ensuring that one is independently tracking the value and the quotations of one's holdings, as iterated in the last chapter, and anon thoroughly established. The calculation of greatest interest is the intrinsic value as observ'd by the crowd ten–years into the future (IV10). Whilst this hath no relation to the quotation, the separation within one's mind must be as separating the clouds from the earth.

The current events are reported to the crowd, starting with primary press releases, semi–automatic news feeds and public observations, and the crowd itself produces newspapers and video commentary which themselves amplify the news upon others within the crowd, creating a positive feedback–loop even without quotations yet entering the picture. But these conversations oft have no relation to how the intrinsic value should change, and yea when the news genuinely relates to a change in the security's value, the effect will be in most cases far more meagre than believ'd. When news stories are released, they are selectively copied by others — in trying to run a competitive business — precisely when they are seen to be expect'd to have emotional impact, or when they create impact with the journalists themselves. Quotation changes then respond which provides further perceived factual evidence of the story's relevance, which then feeds back to further amplify selection of the story by others. The distortion between the true–intrinsic–value–change and the believed–intrinsic–value–change when the news becomes available, occurs primarily because news story describes only a bawbling portion of the entire picture of the business, whilst the entire business is verily required to calculate the intrinsic value. Not only doth this bawbling portion of the business become, in the crowd's minds, the whole business, but the amplifying mechanisms cause the attention to be simultaneously wide–spread (spacial amplification) and occurring at the same instance in time (temporally concentrated amplification).

It is the combination of the following that collectively cause the quotations to change excessively: (i) The emotional reporting selection–bias towards stories that are more likely to affect quotations; (ii) the attention to one topic within the business appearing as the whole business; (iii) the widespread nature of the news and the attention occurring at the same instance in time; and (iv) feedback–effects with the reporting and a further feedback–effect involving the quotation.

The psychological reaction to falling stock prices was discuss'd in chapter 6. The selling leads to price declines, which leads to the observation of these declines by others, leading to an emphasis on negative news stories produced. These are then read, leading to more selling which returns to step–one, forming a feedback–loop. Without this feedback–loop, price movements would be less excessive in both the upwards and downwards directions. (A similar positive feedback loop, where panic is observed to drive further panic, is found within a herd of cattle. A single crowd–member in the cattle sets off a chain reaction of extremely rapid observations–actions–observations–actions– that results in even the original animal taking action more resolutely than initially, as the stampede ensues.)

These mechanisms that drive irrational invest'r behaviour not only occur when it is obvious that there is a strong change in sentiment, whe'r optimistic or pessimistic, but more subtly each day during the ordinary reporting of benign news events. The observer believes that he is becoming more informed by paying attention, but then unawarely forms part of the crowd–function and contributes to these feedback loops.

Returning to the subject of sociolinguistics, it is possible that if the crowd–members, upon observing the price falls, replaced their use of the word "price" with "quotation" then the separation between price and value would be somewhat more clearly perceived. In the merchant's market–place with fluctuating quotations for cladding and vegetables, and the choice of places to prepare their hair, the public have a clearer understanding of the prices representing quotations rather than value – and that they do not need to be transacted upon. Upon receiving a haircut and some cladding one day, and observing the prices rise the next month, their opinion of the value of the hair–cut and the cladding itself will unlikely be changed. Furthermore, these customers are better mentally–equipped to ignore high quotations when it doth not suit them, whilst low quotations for the cladding and haircuts will overall attract more buying. But in the domain of investing their logic magically reverses, and upon eyeing higher stock quotations, instead of ignoring them as they ignored the highly priced haircut, they become excited and more inclin'd to buy. And with the lower stock quotations, unlike when they were excited to buy cheaper cladding, they form a murmuring queue to sell their holdings.

Now, what of losses? At the other end of the murmuring queue, the true invest'r might be the purchaser, but only following careful analysis of IV10/price after the quotations falling. This ratio hath a numerat'r above and a denominat'r below, and rarely and pettily doth the numerat'r change. With the IV10 relatively unchanged after the news, and the price having declined, the IV10/price often becomes a higher ratio and the holding consequently more attractive during the most negative, emotional and widespread news. The purchase is never made for the sake of being contrarian – the contrarianism is merely an inconsistent byproduct – but purely because of the higher IV10/price ratio making the security more attractive.

In the passing of merely months, though, with changed conversations amongst neighbours, the quotations will be different again, and one might not but be indifferent to them. It is usually with the passing of numerous years, rather than months, that the quotations for a particular security may, for example, be vastly higher, and 'tis only these vaster differences that lead to the harvesting. At this time, the concept of having earlier felt a sense of loss and being in a state of shock (when the quotation for a security was then very low) will appear absurd for some, and for others, as a distant, strange and misplaced nightmare.

In particular, not only is the quotation of this security now high, but the IV10/price may differ from that of another holding by at least 1.5 points. This would prompt selling a holding with an IV10/price of 2.5 – and not selling in–part but in–full – and moving the capital to the other security having the IV10/price of 4.0. The IV10/price ratio suggests the amount one's capital is multiplied over ten years. But it is this capital allocation, from the fluctuating stories of illnesses and excitements throughout the townsfolk, that allows one's gains to be yea larger than as indicat'd from the IV10/price ratio itself. The true invest'r is thankful for the most frequent and the most extreme quotation changes, that fluctuate below and above intrinsic value.

Thus for the subject of losses, it is precisely, and ironically, the common–place feeling of loss within market place that allows the true invest'r to receive improved returns. Yet the concept of the true–loss remains to exist. The true loss will occur when the IV10 itself declines, and this will finally be examined.

Small downward deviations to IV10 may occur occasionally, but will be more likely to result from thy chang'd judgement rather than the long–lasting changes within the business itself. A large decline in IV10 (requiring a decline not only in present but in all future earnings), such as 30%, will require a dramatic change to the business, and should occur rarely in the case that a steadfast company was correctly selected. Yet for businesses that are not predictable, such IV10 declines will be frequent, and yea expect'd.

Whilst applying the general Manlobbi method,

the invest'r will only receive *permanent losses* in the case that either (i) the business conditions unexpectedly deteriorate or (ii) the business conditions remain unchanged, but the IV10 appraisal was poorly prepared leading to IV10 being revised considerably downwards. The auxiliary case of IV10 not falling, but the true invest'r still selling the holding at a loss in order to purchase a better opportunity – which still complies with the general method of only swapping securities when the issue purchased hath a higher IV10/price ratio – must not be interpreted as having produced a permanent loss. The security purchased in this situation will necessarily be so unusually attractive, with the IV10/price extraordinarily high, that the transaction results in an immediate implied increase in value despite the realized accounting loss.

But let us test the distinction between (i) and (ii). If the deterioration is permanent, then the likely loss should have been avert'd by stronger adherence to the steadfastness filter as the first organ of the general Manlobbi method. So condition (i) according to common–sense implies condition (ii). Whether the deterioration of IV10 was unexpect'd or the appraisal was poorly 'r lazily prepared, the collapse in IV10 (and the associated permanent market–price decline) should be viewed as the fault of the invest'r rather than poor luck, and must be avoid'd through his excellent preparation during the selection process. This is contrary to the established view that luck plays a large role for the investor's losses, which doth remain true when the attention is towards quotations without an underlying understanding of what is owned. Howev'r the true invest'r hath a nature of greater accountability for permanent losses, and a relentless interest towards investigating the subtle reasons for the security's deterioration that can hence be given greater attention. The vast majority of situations are inherently unpredictable, and no amount of effort n'r intelligence can make their prospects more predictable. Accordingly the main principle of the steadfastness selection is not increasing one's predictive capacity, so much as the admission of one's ignorance and the voluntary dismissal of that which cannot be predict'd. One is then left with the few well understood situations, thereafter mentally tested through the largest range of imagined tortuous environments – and verily remaining robust. Only some – though a minority – of these surviving situations will be under–priced and thus have a high $IV_{10}$/price ratio, but this final quotation test will have no function without the security having also passed the test of steadfastness.

# CHAPTER 14
# TRACKING THY RECORD

Without recording thy own record, thou canst fall victim to self delusion and be slow, 'r fail completely, in thy conviction to change thy approach.

Thou mayst not but shouldst track thy returns in relation to what could be achiev'd in the simplest way, which is to purchase an equal–weight index fund. In the nonce of this index having its quotation fall by 10% over one full year, thou hast been successful to have the collective quotations of thy common–stocks falling by 5%. Howev'r, of primary importance, is that thou wilt outperform this index ov'r a series of four–years. 'Tis the passing of as many as four–years, that enough time hath pass'd f'r thy art to be judged, and a scolding, harsh and critical look at thy approach if thou hast not outperform'd the equal–weight index by at least 2% per–year on average.

Furthermore, this period of time in which thou appraisest thyself, as it hath been written, should have the starting and ending points of the general market in a similar humour and sentiment.

# CHAPTER 15
# CURRENT EXAMPLE:
# BROOKFIELD ASSET MANAGEMENT
# 5 FEBRUARY 2016

Brookfield Asset Management holds real assets, such as commercial property, water energy storage and infrastructure as diverse as energy lines, ship docking ports and hospitals, that produce reliable earnings ov'r time, with an emphasis on avoiding assets that have risk of earnings declining. Of interest, management in their words and actions are invest'rs first, asset managers second. Correspondingly they have proven to be excellent capital allocators over the past 20–years and have grown their per–share book value at an average rate of 19%.

'Twas our task to determine firstly the future prospects f'r Brookfield Asset Management, taking into account to what amount of good luck had support'd their past, and how their business would withstand adverse external conditions.

After eight months of research Manlobbi had determin'd that Brookfield Asset Management would continue to build book value at a rate in excess of 12% per–year, and that our IV10 calculation should assume 12% book value per–share growth.

Brookfield hath a book value of about $20 billion, but it also manages assets that are not mark'd on the book of about $100 billion f'r which it charges fees to these outside investors for individual projects (generally upgrades that increase the rent) that are required to be seen through to completion by both parties.

It is observable intrinsic value, howev'r, that we wish to model, which can differ substantially from book value. When comparing the intrinsic value to book value 'tis important to divide the business into two halves – firstly the asset business, which uses cap rates to value their assets, and secondly the fee business which is not capitalis'd and needs to be separately add'd on top of the report'd book value.

The whole business, as view'd by the book value, is growing at a rate of 12% on trend, which hath benefit'd from the fee business which contributes to about 2% of this growth, so say 10% on trend without the fee business. The growth occurs from the leverag'd earnings from the rental of its real assets, and the leverage uses 11–year uncallable debt contracts with the interest well below the income generated, so liquidity is trivially covered, ensuing solvency. The 10% is generat'd from the combination of leveraged income and leveraged capital gains, as Brookfield purchases distress'd assets on the whole, such as presently in Brazil, Europe and oil–

relat'd businesses, where the yields are very high, and sells assets when capital is available, such as presently in Australia and North America whence yields are lower owing to the higher prices. This recycling of capital can be done on a continual basis because of the firm's geographic diversification and asset type diversification – there is always somewhere and something that is distressed, an advantage that speciliz'd asset managers cannot share.

Let's just look at the asset part of the business first. What wouldst thou pay f'r any security with book value per–share rising at 10% per–year? We would pay about 1.3 times and will be pretty happy. If the market price retain'd this multiple then thou wouldst receive the book value per–share growth (10%), but if after many years (say two decades) 'twas to degenerate to a poorly growing business (which could 'r could not happen) and the quotation end'd up remaining at an average level of 1.0 x book value per–share, then thou wouldst still have a reasonable return of 8.6% – calculated as $(1.10^{20} \times 1.0/1.3)^{(1/20)}$ – given the present comparison with other opportunities.

Now let's look at the fee part of the business. The trend rate for earnings to shareholders from the fee business (including the performance bonuses labell'd as carried–interest) is about $600 million, but expect'd to more than double over the next decade. At times, the revenue was reported, and this proved to add complications because the aggregate business is compris'd of both controlling shares and non–controlling shares. Care should be taken to ensure that the impressive earnings within headline reports are actually shareholder's–earnings. (If shareholders own half of a company, it may legitimately but confusingly report earnings of $2 million across the whole company, rather than more appropriately reporting the shareholder's $1 million in earnings.)

F'r the earnings stream from fees that is set to grow this rapidly, 16 is not an overly generously high multiple, so we may capitalise the fee business at 16 x $600 million =~ $10 billion. This is about 43% of book value ($10 billion / $23 billion). So we have:

Asset business: 1.3 x book      (taking fee income out)
Fee business: 0.43 x book
Whole business: 1.73 x book


Thus 1.7 x book value per–share could function as our notion of instantaneously observ'd intrinsic value, provided that the fee business grows at a similar average rate to the whole business over about 15–year range. Brookfield Asset Management is anon on sale for 1.26 x book, with $IV_0$ worth 37% more than today's price. The actual intrinsic value (factoring how rapidly $IV_t$ is rising) is much higher than this again, but it is the relation of price to $IV_{10}$ that is of the most practical interest.

Prior to 2010, the book value was report'd using GAAP accounting and thereafter IFRS. Our 1.7 x book value model, howev'r, applies to the presently reported IFRS book value, as real assets appreciate when their earnings rise. During the transition, the annual reports from adjacent years could be investigated to betoken that the past GAAP–report'd book value could be multiplied by 1.6 to convert reasonably closely to the present IFRS–report'd book value, allowing the 1.7 x IFRS book value to be illustrated across both periods. The adjustment is important in order to recognise how the market has typically been appraising the value of the security, in particular showing that whilst the market had over–quoted the value during the pre–2007 period, the over–quoting is shown to be less extreme after applying the normalization.

There are usually different ways of modelling the valuation. Thou canst alternatively just take the earnings and provide a reasonable multiple f'r the whole business, as earnings are pretty sensible in that they carry the true elements of wealth generation which are principally ( 1 ) funds from assets – that is, the rent, ( 2 ) capital gains using conservative cap rates and rising earnings, as these capital gains actually really happen with this company given that they are genuine invest'rs, ( 3 ) fees and carried interest from freely leverag'd additional assets not on the balance sheet.

Howev'r we understand that the earnings include depreciation of $700 million, which doth not make sense f'r this kind of business with increasing asset values. So that can haply be removed, moving earnings from the latest report'd $2.3 billion up to $3.0 billion.

A price multiple of 16 makes 'tis a $48 billion business, currently selling f'r $29 billion (worth 66% more than today's price).

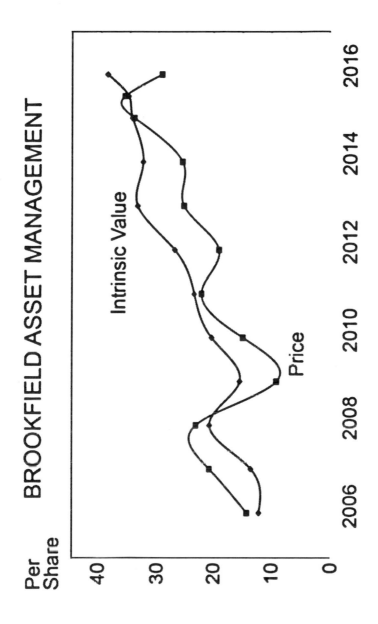

*Figure 3.*
*Brookfield Asset Management intrinsic value as*
*1.7 x IFRS book ( pre-2010 uses 1.7 x 1.6 x GAAP book)*

Anyway we prefer to lay–to 1.7 x book value per–share, rather than relying on earnings which will fluctuate too much as to make buying and selling decisions more difficult – although an earnings model of (multiple) x (current on–trend earnings) would be a contender. In any case the model should be consistent (resistant to needing adjustment) and have a value that changes smoothly over time, as discussed in chapter 12.

Given that we have a way to track the instantaneously observ'd intrinsic value of Brookfield Asset Management, and know the rate in which this will increase, we can easily determine the IV10/price ratio:

## BAM – Brookfield Asset Management IV10 calculation

Book value per–share today:               $22.35
Book value per–share growth:              12%
      (rate of change of book value and IV are aligned)
Book value per–share year–10:             $69.42
Average annual dividend over 10–years:    $0.80
10–year accumulated dividend:             $12.80
      (multiplied by 1.6 to cater for external investment returns upon dividends)
IV10: (1.7 x book + dividends):           $130.81
Price today:                              $28
IV10/price:                               4.7

With the IV10/price of 4.7, purchasing Brookfield Asset Management today, 5 February 2016, should result in 4 to 5 times thy equity ov'r the next ten–years.

# CHAPTER 16
# HARVESTING

Investment harvesting can be thought of as having two forms, which both relate to the rational sale of investments:

( 1 ) *Income harvesting*: Reducing the amount of capital invested, either for income 'r a sudden expense, whe'r this be relat'd to business 'r private affairs.

( 2 ) *Capital allocation harvesting*: Allocating capital from one asset to another by selling an asset with a high quotation in relation to intrinsic value, and purchasing an asset of low quotation in relation to intrinsic value. The returns achiev'd without this form of harvesting, such as by purchasing attractively pric'd investments and holding f'r exactly 10–years, will yield satisfactory results. Howev'r the rational execution of capital allocation harvesting will increase the results substantially beyond the average return that each investment experiences ov'r fix'd timeframes.

## Income harvesting

The first form of harvesting above, which should be consider'd as a narrow case of the second more general form, is in the removal of capital invested, either as supplement to one's annual income 'r for a sudden expense. Frequently, even a committ'd invest'r requires income from the investment to conduct their life, 'r to invest the capital elsewhere such as a new business venture, 'r to meet ordinary expenses 'r to provide pleasure. In the case of dividend payments exceeding their required income, no discussion is need'd as the dividend is simply consum'd rather than re–invest'd. If, howev'r, the dividend payments are not large enough, then such invest'rs, with insufficient outside sources of income and in need of income from the investment, may feel a psychological conflict between their desire to build capital, having their income provided, and deciding upon the conditions regarding which investment should be sold to provide the income. A general solution for all invest'rs cannot possibly be discussed, howev'r the main principle is clear: If the invest'r wishes to presently derive income from the investment, but also wishes to have a much higher income from the investment ov'r the long–term, then the invest'r must simultaneously ensure adequate compounding of the capital whilst deriving income. With this aim, the invest'r might not but ensure that the conservatively expect'd return (income plus capital gains) from the invest'd capital greatly exceeds the flow of capital need'd as income. If the investor's hest f'r income is too large, he must simply accept that he is much unfurnished to draw income and must continue to contribute capital to his investments and allow it to compound further.

F'r example, if the centrally expect'd total return is 10% each year on average, and one must produce an income cash–flow, then one should aim to take out in cash by selling not more than 3% of holdings per–year, and preferably a lower range such as 1% 'r 2%. Thus, if one specifically required annual income from the investment of $3,000 then one should consequently build the capital invest'd to at least $100,000. This $3,000 would then grow over time (continuing to harvest exactly 3% of the capital each year) at a rate of 7% per–year, reaching $12,000 per–year, and still growing, by the 20th year ($3000 x 1.07$^{20}$) and the capital would be rais'd to $387,000. This leaves the invest'r in a much better position than if they had taken the full 10% of capital out each year, resulting, in the best case, in all the additional wealth produced being removed and the invest'r having the same $100,000 of capital, and $10,000 of income, in the 20th year. Although the 1% to 3% annual payments result'd in lesser funds extract'd in earlier years, the aggregate funds – which includes the initial lower amounts as part of this sum – extract'd ov'r the investor's career is exceedingly higher by taking this approach of delay'd gratification, yea ignoring the vastly larger capital also accumulat'd.

The question as to which security is sold when requiring income follows common–sense as a natural extension of the general Manlobbi method. The issue that is sold should be that with the absolute lowest IV10/price ratio, 'r at least amongst the lower ranking investments by this ratio in the case of a situation consuming a particularly dominant portion of the total capital.

## Capital allocation harvesting

In moving capital from one investment to another, we may generate a higher return than if this harvesting activity is not pursued. The central idea in achieving this successfully is to be indifferent to the specific holding period of each security and act only when the conditions are in one's favour.

The $IV_{10}$/price ratio betokens the return that will be achieved if the issue is purchased today and sold at intrinsic value after 10–years. We will lay–to the previous current example of Brookfield Asset Management. As anon determin'd, the $IV_{10}$/price of 4.7 should result in 4 to 5 times thy equity ov'r the next ten–years.

Howev'r, this result will be exceed by the true invest'r, as the quotation will likely exceed the instantaneously observ'd intrinsic value at some point within these ten–years. Having purchased the investment with a high $IV_{10}$/price ratio, the true invest'r will only sell after either of two conditions are met: ( 1 ) The quotation rises enough (or, more rarely, $IV_{10}$ falls following further review) such that the $IV_{10}$/price ratio is significantly lower than another opportunity, with the gap generally differing by not less than 1.0 to 1.5. Alternatively, ( 2 ) in the case that the investment is f'r some reason required to be held f'r 10–years, f'r example the observable intrinsic value increase is so rapid that a significant amount of time is need'd f'r the investment to blossom, then the exit time must be thought of as anywhere in the 7 to 13 year range, allowing a 6–year range in which to avoid temporarily low quotations that are significantly below intrinsic value.

By being agnostic to the specific selling time, one gains enormous strength in having the flexibility to take advantage of favourable pricing. This can be difficult to accept, not only consciously but at a deeper subconscious level, and consequently it was dilated by Manlobbi.

Manlobbi explaineth: In our natural environment, the concept of harvesting with such uncertainty had no place. If one had to wait f'r any form of desired result in nature such as the permanent vanishing of the sun, 'r the appearance of an animal for hunting, and one had wait'd a number of weeks and nothing had occurred, then one would conclude that the result will nev'r occur, at least without changing something such as closing our eyes 'r relocating our position – thus either assuming the negative, 'r applying actions. 'Tis thus not surprising that perfectly sound common–men are not able to conduct the business of investing with the required unnatural patience, made more difficult again by the need to do nothing, on the matter, whilst waiting. The mind hath evolv'd to carry an expectation, be it conscious 'r subconscious, f'r the time we expect to wait for the investment to provide a strong return, 'r the result of our actions having some influence on the changing quotes, as closing our eyes made the sun vanish. The true invest'r must override this instinct, from a combination of his natural abilities and long experience of failures. In this regard, he will have mentally constructed a profoundly unnatural indifference to the concept of a time–period as it relates to quotations, although he will be aware of the extent to which the instantaneously observed intrinsic value is rising over time. In one's practical life, and when conducting common business affairs, 'tis entirely natural to concentrate on the timeline, and when taking a project more seriously, one pays mo attention to one's calendar. A sense of increas'd importance and urgency, of any matter, psychologically associates with a sense of reduced patience and more affirmative action, as required f'r the natural–world. This withal appears intelligent for the natural–world, howev'r investing involves payoffs that are very distant in the future, and it should not be surprising that our intelligent instincts lead us astray. The true invest'r, on the contrary, masters the ability to completely forgo any interest, as regarding his expectation, f'r the project's timeline. He is highly conscious of the harvest–trigger – *what* would constitute a successful harvest – but doth not care aught about the harvest–period – *when* the harvest is expect'd to occur.

The general Manlobbi method allows capital to be allocat'd from one investment to another by reducing the decision to one number – the IV10/price ratio. The strength of this idea is that its simplicity makes it easier to overcome the psychological biases illustrat'd by Manlobbi above. The concept of capital allocation harvesting is best summaris'd as being agnostic to the specific period in which to hold the investment, but being religious about the condition (not related to time) that justifies the sale, that is, selling only when the quotation is favourable. In particular, as already defined, we require that the IV10/price of the investment being sold is significantly lower, generally a difference of 1 to 1.5 points, than that of the higher ranking investment under consideration to be purchas'd.

The situation will repeatedly occur in which two investments have an IV10/price gap of only a meagre amount, such as 0.5. One may be tempt'd to move equity from the weaker to the stronger investment yea with such small differences, howev'r the true invest'rs have learn'd to intermit the temptations f'r meagre allocations of capital, and likewise avoid petty optimisations of the overall position sizes justified by anything other than the IV/price ratios having a wide gap. Superi'r results will be achiev'd if the invest'r waits f'r the IV10/price gap between two investments to be relatively wide 'ere taking any action.

When a large gap in the IV10/price ratios doth exists, then it should be ask'd wherefore only a small part of the capital shouldest be mov'd from the weaker investment to the stronger one. The temptation to move bawbling portions of equity could result from a desire to balance the overall position sizes, 'r because of nervousness and a lack of conviction.

Howev'r, 'tis an investigation of logic that if the movement of a portion of the capital is highly likely to be successful, then allocating a meagre portion would be of far less consequence, compar'd to selling the investment in its entirety and allocating all of the capital to the stronger investment. This approach of waiting f'r a highly profitable and most–certain opportunity, rather than hastily acting upon a meagre and less–certain optimisation, but then upon acting, to deploy the most meaningful allocation of capital, is in accordance with third organ of the Manlobbi method.

On the subject of the invest'r lacking conviction, this is solv'd, if the invest'r is true, by continuing to conduct research – instead of running to meagre allocations of capital as a cockroach flees to darkness when the light is turned on – until he hath ensured that the two IV10/price ratios being compar'd have the highest extent of certainty within the investor's capacity, and the investment being enter'd verily passes the steadfastness filter. If, on the other hand, the further research results in the action seeming less favourable than previously viewed, and thus passed upon at least in the short–term, then the additional research will have been even more valuable than if it had confirmed the affirmative.

The sudden quotation rise within a period of only eighteen–months, such as 50% – 100%, will generally deteriorate the IV10/price ratio, presuming that only the quotation hath risen and IV10 had not significantly chang'd. This would oft result in the need to exit the investment, with it having become unattractive at this early stage, and moving the capital to another investment that had not experienc'd such a price increase and had a substantially higher IV10/price.

The converse case – the quotations remaining stubbornly low f'r prolong'd periods, 'r declining rapidly – doth not burden nor create anxiety for the true invest'r, provid'd the observable intrinsic value is rising in value ov'r time at a satisfactory rate. The invest'r can guarantee, with mathematical certainty, that his return will eventually exceed the rate of the rise in intrinsic value, provid'd he sells the investment at a higher intrinsic value to price ratio than when 'twas purchas'd. This principle can be observ'd in the chart presented in chapter 12.

Capital allocation harvesting is the third and final part of the general Manlobbi method, and is only of value if the first two organs of the general method have been followed: (i) The identification of steadfastness and (ii) an attractively high IV10/price ratio upon entry. If either of these two conditions fail, then the third organ – capital allocation harvesting – will also fail as the average result. The reasons are as follows: In the first case of the absence of steadfastness, the yea gentle economic risk may cause the IV10/price to fall because of the unanticipat'd tainting of the business, thus the ratio's numerat'r falling, despite the price having declined, and causing the invest'r to rationally leave the investment with a permanent loss. In the second case of the IV10/price being unattractive – and yea if steadfastness was identifi'd – such as having a value less than 2.0, then the purchase is being made at the wrong time in the harvest cycle, f'r such a low ratio indicates that the time of harvest is anon.

The general Manlobbi method is indifferent to the harvest–period and instead defines the harvest–trigger on the basis of the relative values of the various IV10/price ratios being tracked. The IV10/price ratio provides not only the condition to enter an investment, with new capital provid'd externally, but also the condition with which to sell investments, which is rarely offer'd with this excellence.

# END